STAYING FOUND

The Complete Map & Compass Handbook

2nd EDITION

JUNE FLEMING

THE
MOUNTAINEERS

Published by
The Mountaineers
1001 SW Klickitat Way, Suite 201
Seattle, Washington 98134

First edition: first printing 1994, second printing 1995, third printing 1996, fourth printing 1997

Published simultaneously in Great Britain by Cordee, 3a DeMontfort Street, Leicester, England, LE1 7HD

Manufactured in the United States of America

Edited by Heath Silberfeld
Illustrations by Jody MacDonald and Jerry Painter
Cover photo by Tom Holt
Cover design by Watson Graphics
Book design, typesetting and layout by The Mountaineers Books

Library of Congress Cataloging-in-Publication Data

Fleming, June.
Staying found : the complete map and compass handbook / June Fleming. —2nd ed.
        p.   cm.
Includes index.
    ISBN 0-89886-397-X
    1. Orienteering. 2. Wilderness survival. I. Title.
GV200.4.F55 1994
796.5'1—dc20   94-10541
                                        CIP

Contents

Taking Off

Map and compass skills are used in various ways, from a competitive meet on a charted course (called orienteering) to the wilderness wanderings of a solitary backpacker. **The goal of this book is to show hikers, backpackers, and other outdoor roamers how to make practical use of map and compass, along with other route-finding skills, in their travels.** It deals with situations and problems they are likely to encounter and provides answers to their particular needs.

> Late at night the tent glows. Heads bend over a map, planning the next day's itinerary. A nameless small lake about 2 miles off the trail looks intriguing. A bearing from camp to the lake is plotted, then inch by inch the squiggly lines, colors, and symbols of the map are deciphered and a likely cross-country route laid out.

> I *know* this compass is broken! Everything's turned around. Some help!

> Sam and Sal find a lovely meadow about a half mile off the main trail. An unmaintained, overgrown trail leads to the clearing, but one could easily pass its junction with the main trail. They want to be sure they can find the takeoff point again.

The hiking friends reach Buck Prairie in the late afternoon. Tents are soon popping up in a circle, doors toward the hub. But there's Carrie, fiddling with her compass in the direction of the setting sun. She's figuring out where the sun will make its morning appearance so she can position her tent to catch the first warming rays.

Wandering away from camp with bird book and binoculars, Neil is engrossed in traipsing after a flock of mountain chickadees. Suddenly it hits—he isn't sure which way leads back to home base.

Jed had a vague recollection... something about the compass needle not really pointing north. "Wish I'd gotten that down pat. Well, I'll just have to ignore it and hike the way the map shows. It's only 1 mile cross-country." A couple of hours later, Jed is stumbling around in a mild panic, a quarter mile off his destination.

Dan is badly hurt. Someone needs to go out for help. Although the ridges enclosing the valley are rugged, there's one easy way over—the notch his party came across the day before. But in the fog no one can see the notch.

Have you ever been in situations like these? They represent just a few of the reasons for mastering the skills of wilderness route finding—the use of map and compass, and countless additional techniques for getting where you want to go in the backcountry and staying found.

Staying found is adequate reason in itself for *really* learning how to get around in the wild. Not just *carrying* a map and compass because they're on every book's list of essential items, but being *absolutely sure* of how to use them to fullest advantage. Each year countless tragedies occur when people get lost in country and situations where they could have stayed found. Many hikers don't know *how* to stay found and, once lost, unwittingly compound their problems and work against being rescued. When searchers eventually locate lost hikers, alive or dead, they sometimes have with them compasses they never learned to use.

Even if you choose to stick to trails, as a skilled route finder you'll always know where you are and what you're looking at. You'll gain a feel for the wider landscape beyond the well-worn path. Knowing you aren't dependent on trails and signs will increase your confidence. Relaxed, you'll see more.

With map and compass as friends, you can explore beyond the tiny portion of wilderness used by those who restrict their travels to popular trails and camps. Your paths and campsites will be pristine, quiet, and private, even on a summer holiday weekend.

A map will become a vivid picture of the land whether you've been to the area or not. Studying it, you can plan trips to suit your needs, see what you want, challenge your abilities to become part of the country, and give your body the kind of workout it's ready for.

With this knowledge, your chances of getting seriously lost are minimized. And when the day comes that you are temporarily disoriented—and it will, if you spend much time in far places—you'll be better able to summon up your resources and see the experience through to a happy conclusion.

Not the least of the benefits to be gained from your efforts is the satisfaction of learning a new and very practical set of skills. Map language, the turns of the compass, and a feel for the lay of the land will add excitement to your travels as they push back your hiking horizons.

Since the payoffs are so great, why doesn't every outdoor person learn route-finding skills? Why do many hikers feel confident with a topographic map but stop short of mastering the compass?

Like many others, I was intimidated by the methods most often used to teach map and compass skills. They included too many formulas to remember, too many separate parts that I couldn't assemble into a useful, orderly whole.

As my outdoor ventures multiplied over the years, the need for way-finding skills grew. Eventually I took those parts of each method that were easiest for me to use, and from them worked out a sensible, easily remembered way to use map and compass together. All procedures start from the same point—one that is easy to learn, and that incorporates the necessary adjustments.

With this unified system it's easy to understand *what*

you're doing and *why*, and, consequently, *how* to do it. It is a visual process, rather than mostly mental. In the classes I've been teaching for years (backpacking, snow camping, wilderness route finding), it's been gratifying to see face after face light up with "*Now* I understand it!" and to know that map and compass work has been demystified for the students. It has taken a place in their stock of accessible, useful skills for outdoor safety and pleasure.

As with *any* system of using map and compass, there are cautions that must be heeded in order to produce accurate results. When the necessary care is taken, this system works at a level of accuracy appropriate for wilderness travel both on and off trails, in all seasons.

There are many types of compasses and many ways of doing map and compass procedures; other books and the instructions that come with compasses treat these options thoroughly. My intention is not to review them all, but to give a clear presentation of the system I've found easiest to learn, apply, and teach, using the kind of compass I consider most practical for hikers. This is the base-plate compass, which has a transparent base plate attached to the compass housing.

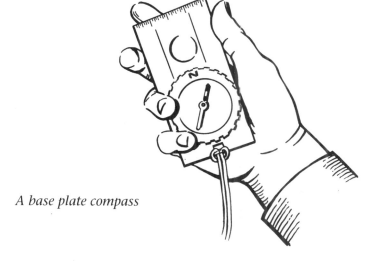

A base plate compass

A Note to Mountain Climbers

Climbers frequently need to use map and compass skills in places that lack level spots on which to lay out their maps. In such situations they might do better to use an alternative method, which is presented in the Appendix (and more fully in *Mountaineering: The Freedom of the Hills*, Fifth edition, edited by Don Graydon and published by The Mountaineers Books, 1992). It doesn't require "orienting the map," so the various procedures (for determining location, identifying mystery features, or deciding on travel routes) can be accomplished by holding the map vertically against a tree or a companion's back. This would also be less awkward in rain.

The major drawback to this alternative method is that, to be accurate, it requires that *exactly parallel north–south lines* be drawn across the map face. Because the only guaranteed north–south lines are the side edges, you need to draw accurate lines *before your outing*—at home, where you have a table and ruler. Additionally, since maps usually have grid lines all over, it may be hard to find yours amid the clutter.

This alternative method is most easily employed using a compass with a built-in declination offset, a feature that adds a few dollars to the cost. Or, you can make a customized declination arrow yourself (see page 49).

The Path Through *Staying Found*

This book is arranged to guide you through use of the basic tools and skills in a way that will be immediately helpful. After an overview are chapters devoted to the fundamentals of maps, compass use, and procedures in which both are used together. "True Directions" teaches how to measure directions in a way that's useful for certain special purposes. "Looking to Nature for Help" shows how the sun and stars, for example, give clues about direction and time. Laying out an excursion either on or off trails is the subject of "Route Planning."

Once you get out there, what can you do with all this? "Staying Found" discusses the dozens of things hikers can do to get where they want to go and to know where they are; it also explains what to do if a hiker gets lost despite best efforts.

"Teaching Kids to Stay Found" presents a whole raft of specific ways to help children develop route-finding skills.

Many people put away their boots come fall and hole up until the spring thaw. But for those wanderers whose appetites are whetted anew by the first snowfall, there's "Route Finding on Snow," which deals with planning where to go on snowshoes or skis, finding your way without many of the usual indicators, and dealing with route-finding problems peculiar to snow-covered landscapes.

Throughout the book I've illustrated instructions with examples from the way-finding adventures of myself and my friends.

Make Things Easy on Yourself

You'll find the information in this book much easier to absorb if you read it with a compass and a topographic map at hand. You should borrow these tools from a fellow outdoor person if you aren't ready to buy your own. The discussion of maps will be even clearer if you can refer to the topographic map of an area you are already familiar with, but for starters any topographic map will do. If you want to get a compass now, skip ahead to page 47 for tips on a good hiker's compass.

What About GPS?

Hand-held Global Positioning System (GPS) units for determining your latitude and longitude are now becoming available. They work in conjunction with orbiting satellites (see Appendix B). As these devices become more affordable, they may become commonplace in the wilds. Wise outdoor users will continue to carry and know how to use a compass, however, in case the electronic fix becomes unavailable due to equipment failure, or should they become separated from the main party.

The Tools of Wilderness Travel

S everal tools can help you get around happily in the outback; they're what th s book is all about. Some, such as technical aids, will be covered briefly now. Others need longer treatment and so warrant an entire chapter.

Without doubt the single most important item in the

toolbox is **you**. A clear, cool head atop a body in good condition, a lively curiosity and adventurous spirit tempered by good common sense—these are indispensable marks of a successful wilderness traveler. The sharpest map and compass user in the woods can still get into big trouble. Technical skills must be used within a framework of active good judgment that continuously sizes up other factors affecting travels: weather, the physical and mental shape of each group member, the group's pace, progress over the terrain, and other matters.

Toolbox Essentials: Map and Compass

Maps are the basis for planning trips and successfully pulling them off. Map talk is so vivid that it can help you estimate the hiking time and difficulty of each leg of your journey, locate water sources, and choose perfect campsites. In an emergency, a map can provide alternate routes to safety. Maps present so revealing a picture of the terrain that it's hard to understand why people ever travel without them. But they frequently do, especially when intending to stay on a popular trail.

A **compass** is a simple device that gives a constant directional reference. Used by itself, without a map, a compass can do the following:

- measure the direction to something you can see, and keep you headed on a straight line toward it even when it disappears from view
- help you get around a big obstacle on your travel line— such as a hill you'd rather go around than over—and pick up your line on the other side of it
- keep you moving straight toward some known baseline such as a road
- help you keep track of changes you make in direction
- guide you to an unseen destination in a given direction
- help you relocate some special place
- tell you where the sun will rise or set
- give you a rough estimate of the time of day

When teamed with a map, a compass will do the following:

- pinpoint your location
- help you identify what you're looking at

- keep you from missing a small destination such as your camp or car
- let you measure, then follow, the direction from one place to another on the map, even if you can't see the goal because of distance or poor visibility

Another part of the toolbox contains **natural route-finding aids**, things that were around long before we hit the trail: the sun, stars, and vegetation. Paying more than casual attention to them can reward you with information about direction and a rough estimate of time, both of which influence your travels.

Extremely helpful **verbal and written information** can be gleaned from diverse sources: the local ranger, friends who have hiked the territory, townsfolk near the trailhead, weather reports, hiking guidebooks, outdoor magazines, trail descriptions. How to get and use these will be covered in "Route Planning."

Some **technical aids** that many outdoor trekkers swear by and others do very well without are binoculars, altimeter, and map measurer. Standard binoculars are a bit too heavy and bulky for most backpackers, so all but the most dedicated wildlife watchers usually leave them at home. For route finding, though, some kind of vision enhancer is beneficial, and you might want to consider an alternative. If you have something that weighs a few ounces and fits in a shirt pocket, you'll use it often. Most outdoor stores carry lightweight, compact **monoculars** ($50 and up) and **binoculars** ($60 and up). If you spend much time outdoors, the pleasure and aid one of these options can give are worth many times the price. They help you roam the wild by assisting with the following:

- making identification of landmarks easier and more accurate—not just peaks and ridges, but your speck of a camp, too
- giving you a clear feel for the overall patterns of the landscape you're exploring
- helping you scout a route visually to avoid dead-end canyons, difficult water crossings, and the like
- showing you alternative routes the naked eye can't adequately assess

Canyon walls that appear uniformly steep and unhikeable, for instance, are frequently threaded top to bottom with animal trails that make for adventurous walking. But you need to know first if the whole wall is passable; getting stymied by an overhanging rim is discouraging after struggling upward for two hours. I celebrated my forty-second birthday climbing out of Southeast Oregon's Blitzen Gorge by such a binocular-scouted route, and was greeted by a soaring golden eagle at the top! The binoculars paid for themselves in one day.

An **altimeter** can help you determine your location by adding an elevation reading to the other things you know. By indicating your present elevation, it can help you decide *where* along a stream or trail you are. It can also tell you when you've reached a contour line on a map and guide you along that line to your goal, minimizing unnecessary up- and downhill climbing.

Because an altimeter is affected by weather changes, an approaching storm can produce a false reading. To get the greatest accuracy, you need to set your altimeter to the known elevation at the trailhead, and reset it frequently at known points as you hike.

Two types of altimeters are available: mechanical (high-quality ones are $150 and up) and electronic ($80 and up). A good altimeter is temperature compensated, calibrated to a high enough altitude to suit your needs, and accurate between 40 and 100 feet; it should display altitude in increments of between 20 and 50 feet.

Altimeters are probably most useful to climbers and other habitual roamers of the high and often trailless reaches.

A **map measurer** ($11) is helpful in trip planning. Set this little gadget down on the map and roll it along your proposed route for a readout on the distance. Realize, though, that to a backcountry walker "a mile" doesn't mean much without other information. In "Route Planning" we'll talk about this and other ways to assess distance on a map.

Maps

Without ever having been to a particular place, and without talking to someone who has, you can already know quite a lot about it.

> The trail begins at the end of a dirt road midway along the north side of a small clearing at 5,600 feet elevation. For the first 0.5 mile we'll climb gradually through trees, curving northeast around a small rise. Off the trail to the right we'll see scattered small meadows with some swampy areas—and possibly the work of beavers? We'd better carry enough water to get us to camp, because the stream we cross at 0.5 mile might be dry. The climbing gets harder as the trail switchbacks up the south ridge of Songdog Mountain, and the view should be terrific when we break out of the trees at 6,800 feet. We'll probably see all the way to Old Whiteface if the weather's good! And we'll be looking down into the Echo Lakes Basin.

The source of all these details is, of course, a map. A map gives a flat, symbolic, bird's-eye view of the earth's surface. Different kinds of maps present different kinds of information, and a hiker may need more than one. This section will tell you how to choose, get, and use the maps you need.

Types of Maps

Highway maps and many maps published by state and federal land-management agencies are **planimetric**, treating the ground as flat. They usually cover quite a large area, accurately place roads and towns, and give rough locations of peaks and large water features. Planimetric maps don't show valleys and hills. In planning a hike, you may need to know where current logging roads are, and their designations, which can change. A planimetric map will often be the best source of current information about these and other manmade features.

Pictorial relief maps give the illusion of showing the shape of the land—its hills, valleys, and such. They can be helpful as aids in trip planning, but aren't sufficient for navigation.

A hiker's best friend is the **topographic** map. By the use of contour lines it gives a detailed picture of the shape of the land—the hills, depressions, flat places, cliffs, and other features you'll need to know about if you explore the land on foot. Colors and symbols on this map indicate whether those hills are wooded or open, where you'll find water, where roads, powerlines, trails, and shelters are located, and many other valuable bits of information. Besides helping you get around in the outback, they're fun to use. From a high spot a topographic map will show you where you've been and where you're going and help you identify peaks and lakes.

Topographic maps are developed by several agencies, but the basic and, generally speaking, most accurate ones come from the United States Geological Survey (USGS). For a given area the U.S. Forest Service or National Park Service may publish a recreational map based on USGS topographic data but updated with information on roads, trails, wilderness boundaries, and such.

USGS maps for many areas are more than twenty years old. If the one for your hiking territory hasn't been revised in the last few years, you should supplement or replace it with a recent topographic map from the Forest Service or another agency that oversees the area. The basic shape of the land is usually a long time in changing, but human "improvements" have speedy consequences.

Most hikers' collections eventually contain several USGS "topos" (also called quadrangles or "quads"), some Forest Ser-

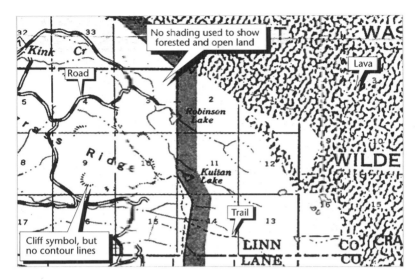

Planimetric map, Forest Service: treats the land as flat and shows only the largest features; shows more current roads, but fewer trails.

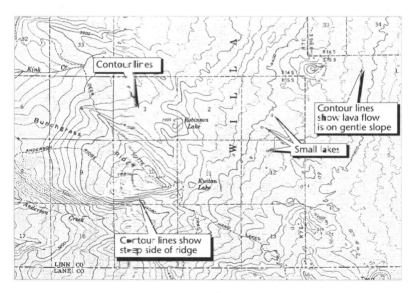

Topographic map, USGS: shows many details of land shape and cover, such as small meadows and lakes and wooded islands in the lava flow.

vice topographic maps of federally designated wilderness areas, National Park Service topographic maps, and planimetric Bureau of Land Management or National Forest maps. A wide range of maps will provide a fuller picture of the place you want to visit, and will also help you avoid errors that cost energy and time.

(In all illustrations from topographic maps we have used a gray screen to indicate what on the actual map is green shading.)

Whichever map you decide to use, be sure it is the *most recent revision*. Rather than assuming a two-year-old map is the newest one, check with authorities. Due to overuse and overcrowding, trails in popular areas are frequently rerouted.

Deciphering a Map

The aim in reading a topographic map is to picture the landforms and features that go with different patterns of contour lines, colors, and symbols. Map-reading mastery will turn the language of squiggly lines, strange marks, and irregular color patterns into a vivid mental image. After a bit of practice in the wild, you'll look at a map and see cliffs, meadows, irregular hills, a notched ridge, a sure water source, a pass that promises a great view. A feel for the shape of the area as a whole will emerge from your "reading" of the parts.

Speaking Topographically

A topographic map's key feature is its **contour lines**, whose patterns make little sense to the untrained eye. Each is an imaginary line on the ground at a constant elevation above sea level. If you trace with your finger a line labeled "6500," everywhere it goes on your map—around a ridge, into a gully, across a glacier—will be at 6,500 feet above sea level. If you could walk that imaginary line on the ground, you'd be walking at a constant elevation, neither climbing nor dropping.

The empty space on the map between two adjacent contour lines represents the elevation change from one line to the next and is called the **contour interval**. The size of this interval stays constant on any one map, but varies from map to map depending on map scale and type of terrain. In flattish country the interval might be 20 feet, but in a mountainous area there wouldn't be room on the map for all the lines if such a small interval were used. More likely the interval would be 40, 50, or even 80 feet On some maps depicting land with little elevation change, broken supplementary contour lines divide the intervals even further.

The interval will be printed at the bottom of your USGS map, or on the legend of other maps, as "CONTOUR INTERVAL 40 FEET." This means that each line is 40 feet above or below the one next to it. Where the lines are jammed close together the land is very steep; you would cover the elevation gain or loss in a short horizontal distance. Where the lines are far apart, you'd walk a longer distance to make the same gain or loss in elevation; the land would be gentler, sometimes nearly flat.

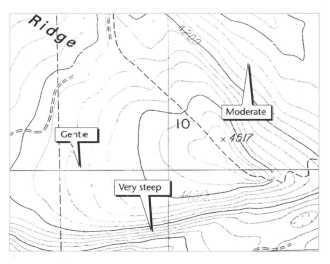

The distance between adjacent contour lines tells how gentle or steep the land is: the closer, the steeper.

Every fifth contour line, called an **index contour**, is darker; its elevation is printed in several places along it. Between pairs of darker lines are four lighter lines. On a map whose contour interval is 40 feet there is a 200-foot change between index lines, a 40-foot change between adjacent contour lines.

By reading the elevations printed along the index contours your trail crosses, you can figure out whether you'll be chugging uphill or sauntering downhill. And by noting how close together the contour lines are, you can gauge the steepness of the slope, as well as the energy and time needed to cover it. An elevation change of 1,000 feet in 1 mile is considered respectably steep.

Keep in mind the contour interval for the map you're using, since a pattern of lines *by itself* doesn't mean much. Four bunched-up lines on a map with a 20-foot interval represent only a 60-foot rise, but the same four-line jam on a map with an 80-foot interval shows a formidable 240-foot cliff!

Checking the contour interval also alerts you that there could be some features the map won't show. What looks gentle could be a series of ledges and slopes. A 60-foot rise or dropoff won't be apparent on a map whose interval is 80 feet. I remember skiing pack-laden through an area that looked invitingly flat on the map but was in reality covered with irregular bumps just under the size of the contour interval, and took twice as long to negotiate as I had planned.

Patterns of contour lines are shorthand for some typical

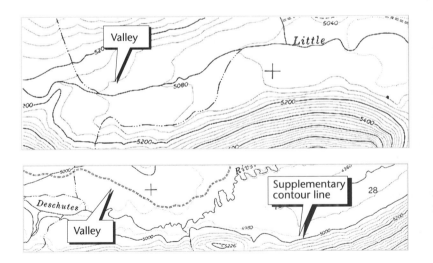

A valley is shown by a pattern of nested U's whose bottoms point to a higher elevation. Sometimes dotted supplementary contour lines add more definition to a very flat area.

landforms. Study these configurations to fix them in your mind; pick them out on several maps; compare gullies and different mountain shapes with their map pictures each time you hike. Soon you'll be translating with ease.

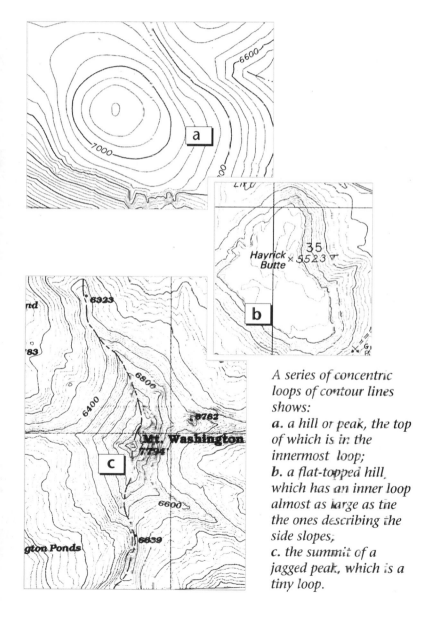

A series of concentric loops of contour lines shows:
a. a hill or peak, the top of which is in the innermost loop;
b. a flat-topped hill, which has an inner loop almost as large as the the ones describing the side slopes;
c. the summit of a jagged peak, which is a tiny loop.

A closed circle or loop can also be a depression, indicated by tick marks inside the loop.

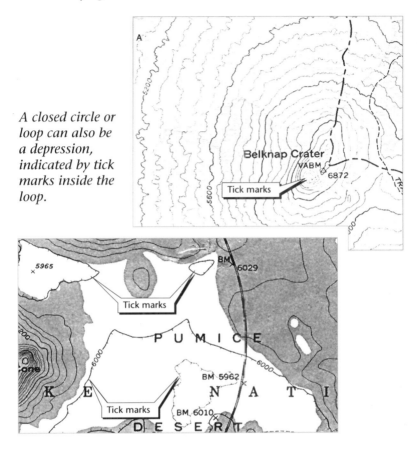

Two U-shaped sets of lines meeting bottom to bottom denote a saddle or pass between two higher areas.

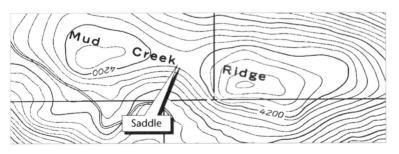

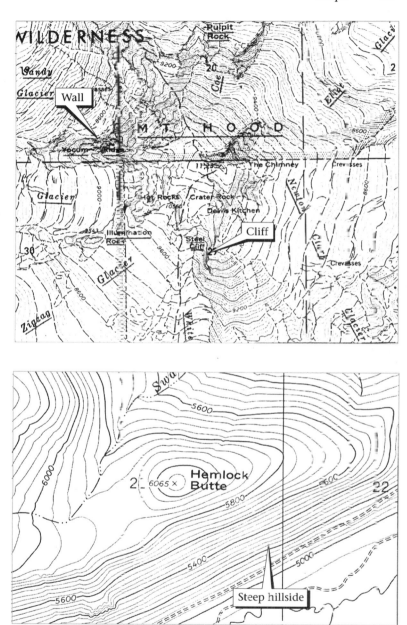

Lines very close together indicate a steep wall, cliff, or hillside.
Elevation change is great within a short horizontal distance.

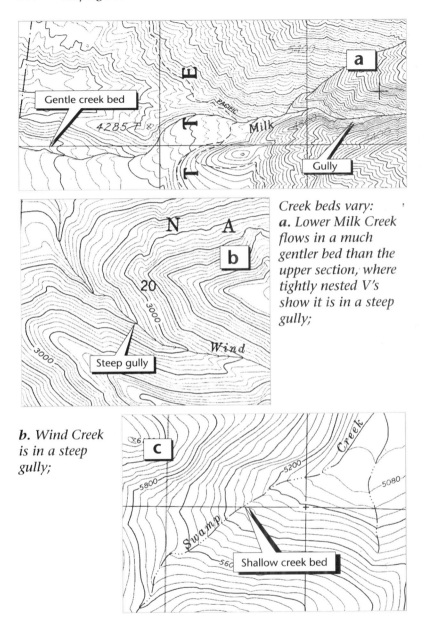

Creek beds vary:
a. Lower Milk Creek
flows in a much
gentler bed than the
upper section, where
tightly nested V's
show it is in a steep
gully;

b. Wind Creek
is in a steep
gully;

c. Swamp Creek's bed is in a nest of broad U's, showing that it
barely dents the hillside.

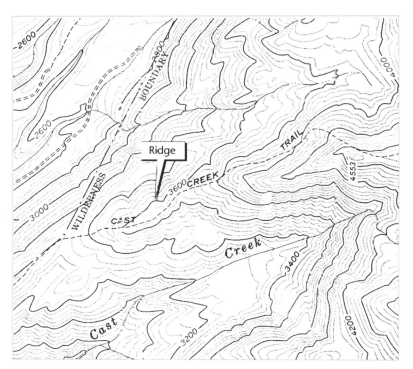

A ridge appears as a downhill-pointing nested set of U's or V's, depending on the sharpness of the crest. Cast Creek Trail follows the ridge in the center of the map.

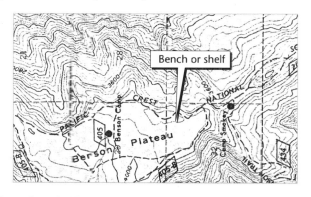

A bench or flat shelf in otherwise steep terrain is pictured by parallel lines that suddenly spread apart. Benson Plateau is a flat shelf atop a steep-sided hill.

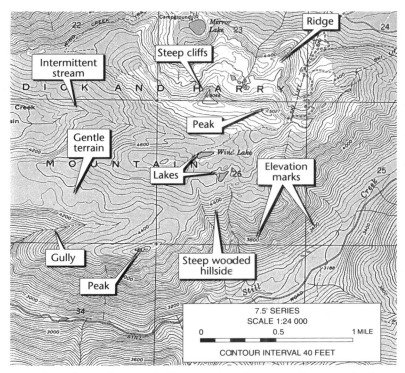

Together, the scales, symbols, patterns of contour lines, and colors of a topographic map provide much valuable information.

Five **colors** are used on USGS maps. (Please refer to an actual map—the samples in this book do not show colors.)

green	*Solid overprint for tree cover, irregular dots for scrub.*
white	*Untreed. Surface can be almost anything except trees or water: grassy, barren, with sand, small rocks, large boulders.*
black	*Manmade features such as campgrounds, roads, buildings,powerlines, trails, shelters; county, state, National Forest boundaries; names, some elevations.*
brown	*Contour lines, their elevations, some peak elevations.*
blue	*Water features and names, including oceans, lakes, glaciers, swamps, springs. Perennial lakes and streams, which contain water all year, have solid lines; intermittent or seasonal ones are shown by broken lines. Contour lines of glaciers and permanent snowfields are shown in blue.*
red	*Some roads, urban areas, and U.S. land-survey lines.*

Photorevised maps will show changes with a **purple** over-print, but these revisions usually cover urban areas. A hiker isn't likely to find purple markings on a map, except perhaps depicting road changes nearby.

Symbols can be either pictographs that resemble the objects they stand for or abstractions, and in both cases they are printed in colors consistent with their meaning. The tadpolelike sign for a spring will be blue, as will the bunches of vegetation indicating a swamp or marsh. Two colors in conjunction describe the feature and its setting. For instance, a marsh in a clearing is pictured by the blue marsh symbol on a white background; if the marsh is submerged, both symbol and background are blue.

Elevations are noted in ways that indicate how the figure was obtained. While interesting, the distinctions are not usually vital to hikers. What *is* important is that marked elevations can help foot travelers confirm or figure out their location.

Particular spots on the map (often high places, but not always) may be marked with the elevation and an x, BM, or VABM, and sometimes a triangle with a dot in it. These symbols are called **benchmarks**. If you go to the benchmark site, you'll probably find a permanent metal marker with the elevation printed on it. If this marker is in a brushy spot there might be a tree blaze or a paint spot on nearby rocks to help locate it.

Map elevations printed in black have been field checked; those in brown were taken from earlier maps but not field checked. Some elevations were actually verified on foot; others were calculated from aerial photos or visual sightings from other points of known elevations. Don't confuse the x of an elevation mark with the larger "plus" signs that divide the map in thirds vertically and horizontally (along with tick marks on all four sides).

Directions. Maps are laid out with the top toward the top of the earth—true north, also called "geographic north" and "map north." The side edges are the *only* lines on the map guaranteed by the mapmakers to run true north–south.

Coverage and scale. USGS topographic maps are bounded by parallels of latitude (east–west) and meridians of longitude (north–south), oriented to the geographic north pole, the upper end of the earth's axis. Latitude and longitude of the area

Paved road	
Light-duty road	
Unimproved road	
Railroad	
Power line with located metal tower	
Buildings	
Trail	
County boundary line	
Township or range line (red)	
Section line (red)	
Elevation marks	×5466 △3112 BM × 7018
Index contour	5200
Intermediate contour	
Supplementary contour	
Perennial streams	BLUE
Intermittent streams	
Spring or seep	
Water well	(blue)
Small falls	
Marsh, swamp	
Woods	SOLID GREEN
Scrub (green)	

Common map symbols

enclosed by a map are printed at each corner in degrees (°), minutes (') and seconds ("). Sixty minutes equals one degree. (Since all the meridians of longitude on the globe converge at the poles, do the north–south margins on our topographic maps also converge? Yes, a tiny fraction of an inch, not enough to cause significant errors in route finding.)

Maps are available in several series, but three are most useful to foot travelers. The 7.5-minute series maps (scale 1:24,000) cover 7.5 minutes of latitude and longitude, an area of 49 to 71 square miles, on a sheet of about 22 inches by 27 inches. (Coverage depends on latitude; the closer an area is to the equator, the more square miles the map will cover.) Maps in the 7.5 x 15-minute series (scale 1:25,000) cover 98 to 140 square miles on sheets measuring about 24 inches by 40 inches. Maps in the 15-minute series (scale 1:62,500) cover 197 to 282 square miles on a sheet about 18 inches by 22 inches.

A 7.5-minute map covers one fourth the area of a 15-minute map and is printed on a slightly larger sheet of paper; it is easier to read and offers more detail. But it has a drawback: if a person needs to identify a landmark more than a few miles away, it will likely be off the map. Also, if a lost hiker can spot only one recognizable hill and it is too far away to be on the map in hand, this knowledge can't be used to pinpoint position. Clearly, these maps don't give a broad picture of the land. Yet carrying all the adjacent maps can be cumbersome.

One solution is to use both—the 7.5-minute map for your main area of travel and the 15-minute or a Forest Service topographic for the bigger picture. Another is to supplement your 7.5-minute map with a 1 x 2-degree series (scale 1:250,000) USGS map (published for most areas). An inch on a map of this scale equals about 4 miles and the map will cover enough territory to encompass most landmarks you'll see (4,580 to 8,669 square miles; it would take thirty-two 15-minute maps or 128 7.5-minute maps to cover this same area!).

A 15-minute map includes many more landmarks than a 7.5-minute map, and although there's a bit less detail shown, the scale is certainly adequate for foot travel. There isn't always a choice of scale—15-minute maps are being phased out—but when both are available, you'll have to decide which suits your needs best. On a trip of more than a day or two, you will probably walk across a whole 7.5-minute map; a weeklong ramble could cover several. An Oregon backpacker traveling the state's 498-mile portion of the Pacific Crest Trail migrates across thirty 7.5-minute maps. (Fortunately, the Forest Service condenses strip maps of the trail into three brochures.)

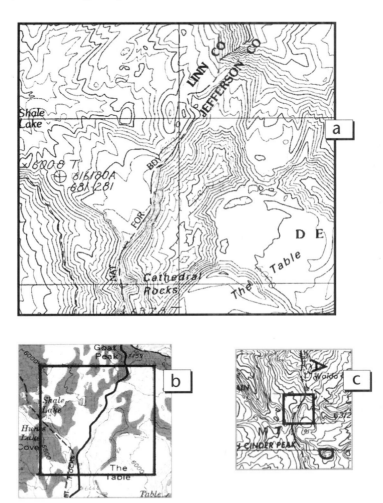

*The same area in three scales: **a.** 7.5' map (contour interval 40 feet) shows greatest detail; **b.** 15' map (contour interval 80 feet) has less detail, but enough for foot travel; **c.** 1:250,000 map (contour interval 200 feet) shows only the largest details.*

The **scale** of a map is noted in the legend (lower margin of a USGS quad) and describes the relationship between distance on the map and corresponding distance on the ground. Scale is usually stated as a ratio. A 15-minute map has a scale of 1:62,500, meaning one inch on the map equals 62,500 inches on the ground. Roughly translated, this means one map inch covers about 1 mile. Very handy! On 7.5-minute maps the scale is 1:24,000 and 1 mile of ground is pictured by about 2.5 inches of map.

Bar scales printed with a map's legend give a means of measuring distance on the map in kilometers, meters, miles, and feet.

Miles or kilometers? Generally, distances and elevations on 1:24,000-scale maps are given in conventional units (miles and feet) and on 1:25,000-scale maps in metric units (kilometers and meters).

Provisional edition maps are made in 1:24,000 or 1:25,000 scale (1:63,360 for Alaska 15-minute maps) in conventional or metric units and either a 7.5 x 7.5-minute or 7.5 x 15-minute format. Map content is generally the same as for **standard edition** maps. However, modified symbolism and production procedures are used to speed up publication of these large-scale maps. As current maps are revised, they are produced in the larger scale; these will eventually replace all 15-minute maps. At some future time, provisional maps will be updated and reissued as standard edition maps.

Privately produced and Forest Service maps that are specifically designed as recreation guides often print mileage figures along the dashed lines, for sections of trail between dots or arrows. Some maps also print the name and/or number designation of a trail along its line.

More Map Features

A map is **named** for some prominent feature within its bounds, with name and series printed at both the top and bottom of the sheet. If your route goes beyond one map, you'll need to know the names of **adjoining maps**. Older USGS maps put these names in parentheses on all four corners and sides. Newer editions provide a grid of adjoining quadrangle (map) names in the lower margin, along with the map's location in its state's outline.

The **date** a map was originally issued is found under its name at the bottom, but even more important is the date of the most recent field check, found at the lower left. Information on the map was accurate as of that year, but many changes could have occurred since. If the map is outdated, you may hike across unforeseen roads and powerlines, or search in vain for a trail long since abandoned and overgrown or a spring gone dry. Meadows and clearcuts fill in with trees, avalanches smash through timbered mountainsides, swamps become ponds, shelters are built or torn down. Make sure you have the latest word, whether by talking with someone familiar with the area or by checking a more recent map put out by the agency that oversees the land (Bureau of Land Management, Forest Service, Park Service, state agencies).

Another vital piece of information is found in the map's bottom margin: the area's **magnetic declination**. Older maps have an angle diagram with the declination number printed to the side. Newer maps give declination in the lower left-hand corner. You must know declination in order to use map and compass *together*. Of course, a map can often be used alone with reasonable accuracy when visibility is good. For further explanation of declination, see Chapter 5, "Putting Map and Compass Together."

As noted above, boundaries of counties, states, national forests, and national parks are usually printed in black with names on either side of the lines. Trails are also shown in black—by dashed lines—so make sure you don't plan to hike a county line.

Kilometer grids in black cover newer USGS map editions; they provide a quick way for metric-thinking hikers to estimate distance. Caution: the vertical lines do *not* run true north–south.

Red vertical and horizontal lines frequently divide most or all of a map (including USGS and topographic maps issued by other agencies) into squares with red numbers in the center. Caution: the vertical lines seldom run true north–south. These **U.S. Public Land Survey System lines** assist hikers in both route planning and staying found. The lines were developed to divide land into units 1 mile square called **sections**. Thirty-six sections are grouped into a larger square called a **township** and the sections are numbered in a back-and-forth pattern beginning at the top right corner.

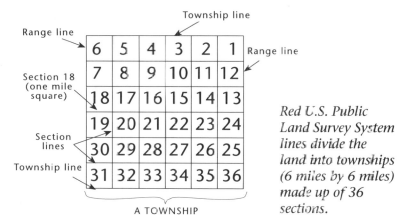

6	5	4	3	2	1
7	8	9	10	11	12
18	17	16	15	14	13
19	20	21	22	23	24
30	29	28	27	26	25
31	32	33	34	35	36

A TOWNSHIP

Red U.S. Public Land Survey System lines divide the land into townships (6 miles by 6 miles) made up of 36 sections.

Townships are stacked in rows set off by vertical lines called **range lines** and horizontal lines called **township lines**. Small red letters and numbers along all four sides of the map refer to range and township designations.

Because each section is 1 mile square, it provides a quick estimate of distance on a map. And when you and a friend discuss an upcoming trip, you can use section numbers for ready reference: "How about exploring the long canyon in section 31?"

Land survey divisions sometimes help you confirm your location, even get you found. There is frequently a **marker** set where section lines intersect; you can read the location from the marker and pinpoint it on your map. At some section cor-

A hiker at a bearing tree figures out his location by comparing Land Survey designations on the metal plate with those on his map.

ners the marker is a yellow metal plate printed with the numbered sections, also noting range and township numbers. A nail through the plate marks where you are.

The type of section corner marker used depends on when the land was surveyed and how much disturbance there has been since by fire, avalanche, human acts, or other derangements. It's still possible to find markers from surveys done in the 1800s, when a corner might have been designated by notches chipped into a large native stone, a blaze or sign on a "bearing tree," or a notched post.

Not all lands have been surveyed, so if you're exploring a wilderness area or national park you might never encounter public land survey system markers. In such places, elevation benchmarks may be the only permanent evidence of survey work. (Occasionally a hiker encounters a post or stone marked during a mineral survey—MS followed by a number—but these probably aren't on the map.)

But There Are Limits

A topographic map can tell you much about the land, but not everything. Some limitations have already been mentioned: not showing terrain features if their elevation difference is less than the contour interval; not registering recent changes in trails, roads, vegetation, or land shape.

Another hitch is that you can't always judge how difficult a piece of terrain is by reading contour lines and colors. What the map indicates as a barren, formidably steep draw could be a negotiable scree slope offering relatively stable footing.

On a topographic map, white means simply that the area is free of trees and scrub, not what it *is* covered with—information that affects your travel even if there's a trail. You could be in for a trudge across sand, gravelly rocks, tippy plate-sized slate slabs, big boulders to hop or weave through, grassy clumps on little hillocks, smooth flat "lawn," or endless variations on the treeless theme. Some of the variations could make off-trail travel extremely difficult and hazardous, or even impossible.

There are a couple of situations in which a map alone cannot get you where you want to go or keep you found. The obvious one is when thick woods or darkening weather limit visibility. Certain types of country are hard to figure out without the added help of a direction finder. Both monotonous hill country and areas filled with lakes have so many similar features that you can't tell one hill or lake from another just by studying the map. (Enter the compass!)

Sources of USGS Maps

USGS maps are sold in many outdoor stores (some also stock National Forest and wilderness maps), some bookstores, travel stores, and other retail outlets (look in the Yellow Pages under "Maps"). Further, the USGS has thirteen offices that offer nationwide information and sales of USGS maps. For addresses of these and state USGS offices, call 1-800-USA-MAPS.

You can also order maps by mail from the addresses below. To figure out which map you need, call 1-800-USA-MAPS and request a free index and companion catalog for the state in which you plan to hike. This lists all available maps on a chart printed over the state's outline, as well as special maps—of national parks, for example—published for the area, addresses of local map dealers, map reference libraries, and federal map distribution centers. When you request an index, also ask for the free folder "Topographic Map Symbols."

Order the map you want by name, state, and series/scale. Enclose a check or money order payable to the Department of the Interior–USGS. A $1 00 postage and handling charge should be included on orders of less than $10. Send your order and prepayment to the following:

USGS Map Sales
Box 25286
Denver, CO 80225

If you have questions, call 303-236-7477. The 7.5-minute and 15-minute maps are a bargain at $2.50 each; prices of other maps are listed in the index.

Alaska residents may order maps and indexes directly from:

USGS Map Sales–Alaska
U.S. Geological Survey
101 Twelfth Avenue, Box 12
Fairbanks, AK 99701

The USGS has a very helpful central information source

that gives prompt, clear answers to any map-related questions you might want to ask. Call or write to the following:

Earth Science Information Center
U.S. Geological Survey
507 National Center
Reston, VA 22092
1-800-USA-MAPS

Canadian Maps

Three free indexes list what's available from National Topographic System Maps of Canada. Order the index and whatever maps you want from the following:

Canada Map Office
615 Booth Street
Ottawa, Ontario
Canada K1A 0E9

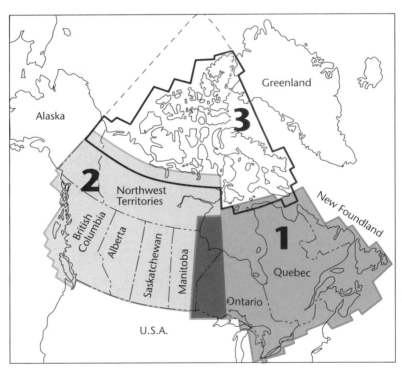

Index zones for Canadian maps

This office will also send a listing of provincial topographic map dealers, and a list of dealers outside Canada from whom individual maps may be bought.

Other Maps

In addition to USGS topographic maps, you may want to get more recent maps put out by the agency managing your hiking area. In most of the United States the wild places sought by foot travelers are controlled by one of four federal agencies: the Forest Service, the National Park Service, the Fish and Wildlife Service, or the Bureau of Land Management. A few states have more hikeable country that is state-owned: New York, Maine, Michigan, Wisconsin, Alaska, and California.

The Forest Service has planimetric maps of its national forests, national grasslands, and some national parks, and topographic maps of the designated wilderness areas within its territory. Maps cost $2 and up. There are nine regional offices and, within each region, maps are also available at forest supervisors' offices and district ranger stations. The addresses of these places are listed in your phone book under "United States Government, Department of Agriculture."

The Bureau of Land Management has ten regional offices and oversees mainly desert terrain in the West and Southwest. The Fish and Wildlife Service, with seven regional offices, is in charge of wildlife refuges. These two agencies, along with the National Park Service (eight regional offices), are listed under "United States Government, Department of Interior."

Private firms often produce topographic maps intended mainly for hikers, cross-country skiers, and snowshoers. These are based on the USGS topographic data and emphasize trails. Some maps add shading for pictorial relief, which makes it easier to visualize the terrain. The maps are sold at outdoor, travel, and some book stores.

Use and Care of Maps

Maps are cheap and easily replaceable from your home base, but not in the outback, so take care to keep them in usable shape. A soggy map is soon unreadable.

Many travelers fold the portion in use outward and carry

the map in a one-gallon plastic ziplock bag. Heavier and more durable map cases are sold at outdoor stores. With either of these, you can consult the map without exposing it to the elements.

Spray-on and paint-on waterproofing products sold in outdoor stores are minimally effective, for a short time. For a map you use often, a more permanent, slightly heavier, and bulkier alternative is to cover one or both sides with clear Con-Tact® paper (sold in houseware departments by the roll, along with the printed stuff used to cover shelves). This method does a better job of preserving what's on the folds, makes your map absolutely waterproof, and is especially good for rainy or snowy treks. (Draw bearings on coated maps with an indelible felt-tip pen; erase them with an alcohol swab.)

Maps can also be cut into sections and backed with dry mounting cloth (available at engineering supply outlets) in a somewhat more tedious process that produces a durable sheet.

If your route covers two adjoining maps, you can trim margins where they meet and tape the maps together from the back. Caution: save any marginal information you might need, especially from the bottom legend, and transfer important data to the backs of the maps.

Occasionally your hike might cover territory at the corners of two to four maps. Cut and join these sections into one map that gives you a readier glimpse of the whole area, being careful to match contour lines at the edges and to write on the back of each piece the name and date of the original map.

If your trip is long, your pack crammed full, and your mind bulk conscious, it's easy to get carried away with trimming and leaving adjacent maps home. *Don't overdo it!* To save bulk and weight on a long ski trip through Crater Lake National Park, we lifted from the center of the map just the small part our route covered. When we tried to identify landmarks just a few miles away, we bemoaned our economy.

What Can You Do With a Map?

As long as visibility is good and the country well defined, with *map alone* you can answer the same basic questions you could answer more precisely with map and compass: Where am I? What am I looking at?

The best way to learn map reading is to spend time leisurely in an area you know well. In the same way that you might take a hike specifically to watch birds or learn to identify mushrooms, take one to study maps.

Compare what you see with its picture on the map. Start with the most prominent features: peaks, large clearings, lakes, drainages. Then carefully decipher the less obvious: smaller hills, ridges, streams. You won't get it all down firmly on one hike, but every bit of practice will help you visualize from the map patterns and symbols and develop a sense of scale about distances and elevations.

Always remember that maps show a bird's-eye view. Since we're not ravens soaring above the land, what we see is limited by our land-based perspective. Just because you can see something on a map, don't assume you can *actually* see it. When you look at a hill, for instance, you see only the portion of its map picture that is toward you and not hidden by something else.

Matching Map and Landscape

As long as visibility is good and you can identify a couple of landmarks, you can line up your map without a compass. This is called "orienting by visual inspection" and is done by sighting across landmarks on the map to their counterparts in the terrain.

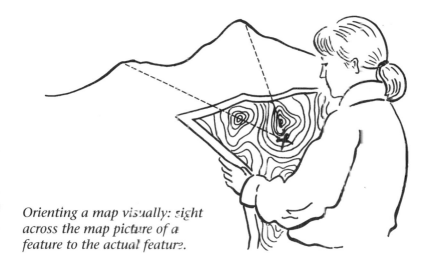

Orienting a map visually: sight across the map picture of a feature to the actual feature.

Orienting the map visually (or with the greater precision afforded by a compass) connects hikers to their surroundings, helps them see the larger picture, and their place in it. Hikers who nurture this habit are usually both safer and more appreciative of the places they're exploring.

How Far Away Is That Mountain?

An ability to judge distances accurately is not a natural gift, but it is a route-finding skill worth developing. Judging distances accurately can help you identify features and avoid quick (but wrong) assumptions that could lead to trouble. ("We must be almost to camp... that's got to be Cougar Rock ahead.")

Practice this skill frequently each time you use a map. Look around for a known feature—say a lake or a peak—and guess how far away it is. Now lay a string (or any straightedge) on the map, starting at the feature and going through your location. Pinch off the string with thumb and index finger at that spot. Now lay the measured string along the bar scale in the map's legend, being careful to begin where "0" is marked. It's not usually at the left end, but in the middle or elsewhere along the bar. How close was your guess?

Be aware that several factors influence your judgment about how far away a feature appears to be: its color, the amount of contrast with the background, and the air between you and the feature. In general, dark objects appear closer than light ones. Whatever the feature's color, if it contrasts sharply with the background, it will seem closer than if there is little or no contrast. A tree-clad hill set against others of its kind will seem farther away than would a bare, rocky hill in the same setting. A snow-covered peak appears more distant on an overcast day than it does against a blue sky. How clear or hazy the air is between you and the feature also affects your ability to judge distance. Clear air makes things look closer than when they are viewed through haze or mist or smog.

What Am I Looking At?

If you know where you are and can orient the map as above, you can identify unknown landmarks around you. Line up your map, then put one end of a straightedge (the longer the better)—a stick, ruler, pencil, another map folded, edge of a notebook—on your map location and point the other end at the actual feature you want to identify. Keeping the straight-edge pointed at the feature and anchored at your location, lower it onto the map. If it isn't long enough, extend the line it makes by overlapping another straightedge a couple of inches (overlapping keeps the line straight). Study this line of sight on the map to see what similar features it passes through.

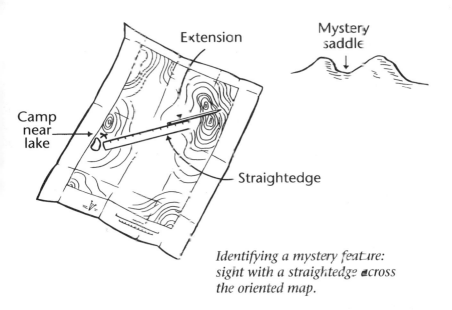

Identifying a mystery feature: sight with a straightedge across the oriented map.

Carefully compare the landmark shapes, tree-cover patterns, elevations, and distances from you with the unknown feature. Don't assume that the tallest peak in a line is the one you see. If you're close enough to a lower peak, it can obscure a taller one behind it.

When trying to identify anything, always beware of that common human tendency to call things what we want them to be (particularly when we feel anxious or lost). If you are almost sure you're looking at Forked Butte, you may hastily misidentify Rabbit Ears, ignoring small but telling details such as rock-slide areas or one of the twin summits being slightly higher than the other.

Which Is Mount Magnificent?

You know where you are, and perusing the map tells you that Mount Magnificent should be in view from here. You can see several peaks that might be it. To find out which one it is, orient your map, then lay a straightedge on the map so that it touches both your location and Mount Magnificent. Sighting along the straightedge and, in an extension of that line, across the terrain, you'll see that mountain and maybe some others. Closely relate their shapes, relative elevations, and distances from you with the map to decide which one is Mount Magnificent.

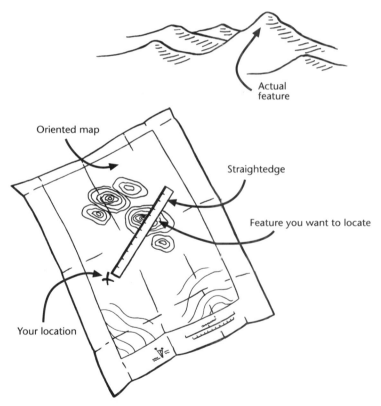

Determine which of several features is the one you want by using a straightedge and your map.

Where Am I?

One very helpful bit of map work is discovering your location by sighting on known landmarks, which is called **triangulation**. Later we'll see how to do this more precisely with the aid of a compass, but in good visibility the same basic procedure done with map alone can give you a rough estimate of where you are.

If you know you are somewhere on a given line such as a trail, stream, or ridge, then you can plot your approximate location by sighting or just one known landmark. Orient your map by lining it up with known terrain features, being careful not to move the map while you then make your sightings. Put one end of a straightedge on the symbol of an identifiable landmark and point the other end at the actual landmark. Lower the straightedge onto the map, checking to keep it pointed at

Pinpoint your location along a line (such as a trail) by a straightedge sighting on one known feature.

the known feature. Extend the line made by this pointer toward you by putting a second straightedge on the map along the line of sight. Where this line crosses your trail, stream, or ridge is where you are. If you can make a second sighting on another known landmark—preferably around 90 degrees, or a quarter-circle away from the first—you'll have an even more accurate "fix."

What if you have no idea where you are but can see and identify two landmarks? Simply take sightings with straightedges, as above, and plot the lines of sight on your map. Where the lines intersect is your approximate location. And again, three sightings can pinpoint it even better.

Remember that there are some situations in which a map alone isn't sufficient to guide your travels or keep you from getting lost: in limited visibility due to weather or trees, and in certain kinds of terrain—rolling wooded hills, or dozens of similar lakes. Then you need the added help of a direction finder.

The next two chapters describe, respectively, several basic procedures with a compass alone and methods that use map and compass together.

Compass

This simple palm-sized gadget, with so few parts that you can count them on your fingers, has bailed out many a bewildered hiker.

Compass in his pocket, a Scout leader left base camp to go out for supplies. Because the trail was "clear" he took no map. On his return trip the trail became vague where it reentered the woods after crossing a meadow. My friend veered slightly in the wrong direction. Slightly is all it takes; after a half mile, nothing looked familiar. Resisting that sinking feeling, he climbed a high spot and cased the terrain until he recognized a rockpile he had noticed near camp. A compass bearing to the rockpile gave him a straight line to travel. Home again, with the goods!

This comforting device also makes possible wanderings that otherwise would be foolhardy.

For two days a steady snowfall hid from view all the spectacular scenery we knew was there: frozen lakes, big and little hills, one stunning peak. Sure, it was disappointing not to be able to see anything beyond a quarter mile or so, but we had a grand time anyway, skiing up and down and all over an area about 4 miles square. Until the afternoon we headed home, we never knew our exact location. Were we worried? No, because our prior knowledge of the country, combined with a compass, kept us found; we used a baseline. A conveniently placed highway ran east–west, and we were skiing north of it. So wherever we were, heading south would take us to this road. Sure enough, we eventually topped out on a rise and spotted an identifiable lake, a bit north of the highway and 2 miles east of the car.

Those of us who stray off streets and highways need an artificial direction finder simply because we aren't naturally equipped with one. We can rely to some extent on natural aids like the sun, and on landmarks when we can see and recognize them. But with a compass our ranging isn't restricted to familiar territory or clear days; we can change from passive tourist to active explorer.

A compass is basically a magnet mounted on a pivot, free to turn in response to the pull of the earth's magnetic field. The housing protects the needle and helps you relate the direction in which the needle points to directions on the map and on the land. A compass by itself can't tell you where you are or what you're looking at, but it *can* tell you about direction—which is a lot more than your instincts can do.

What Makes a Good Hiker's Compass?

There are dozens of styles and models of compasses, designed for different uses. A hiker doesn't need to pay for or cart around the elaborate, precise, costlier, heavier compass a surveyor needs.

The base-plate compass designed in Sweden in the 1930s has several features helpful to a wilderness route finder. It's the type of compass most often sold in outdoor stores (Silva and Suunto are the main manufacturers) and most often carried by hikers. Its unique design makes compass operations so simple that hardly anyone fiddles with the old round pocket compass anymore. The price is reasonable and the product durable and functional. Helpful features include the following:

- a rotating housing with both cardinal points (N, E, S, W) and degrees (0–360) marked clockwise on the rim, with intermediate degree marks every two degrees (every five degrees is too hard to work with)
- a liquid-dampened needle whose north-seeking end is red or marked in some other clear way
- a transparent base plate on which the housing is mounted (longer base plates yield more accurate bearings), with a direction-of-travel arrow for sighting and following bearings, and straight edges that make it easy to measure and plot directions on a map
- a built-in magnifier to help identify small map symbols and read small or faint print
- an orienting arrow printed on the bottom of the housing; its north end usually red

Compasses with the above features come in several models and cost $9–$20.

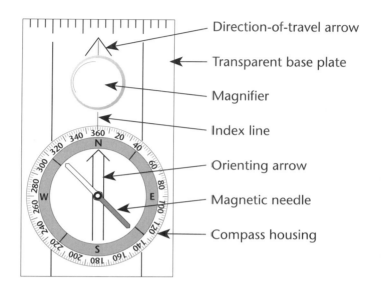

Direction-of-travel arrow

Transparent base plate

Magnifier

Index line

Orienting arrow

Magnetic needle

Compass housing

Parts of a standard hiker's compass

Some base-plate compasses have hinged mirrors with sighting notches; the notch and line across the mirror function as the direction-of-travel arrow. These compasses are said to be more accurate for measuring bearings. Perhaps most people find this true, but I find it difficult to accurately align the magnetic needle with the orienting arrow when holding the compass at eye level as recommended. When you shop, try both the flat and hinged-lid types to see which works best for you. Mirror-sighting compasses cost $24 and up.

An optional compass feature that adds to the cost is an adjustable declination offset ($28–$40). The method of adjusting for declination in Chapter 5, "Putting Map and Compass Together," doesn't require this feature. For alternative methods taught elsewhere, including the one presented in the Appendix of this book, an offset mechanism may be desired.

Sometimes (as when orienting map with compass, page 82, and when using true directions. page 96) this book will instruct you to point the magnetic needle at the declination number on the compass dial. To do this a bit more easily and precisely, you can add a taped declination arrow yourself.

Here's how: use masking tape or a scrap of opaque Con-Tact® paper to make an arrow the same width as the orienting arrow, and long enough to extend from the inside of the compass dial across the central pivot point. Cut a point exactly mid-width on one end. Affix this tape arrow carefully to the underside of your compass so that its point is at the number of your declination and the shaft goes straight across the central pivot point.

Deflection

Because a compass needle aligns itself with the earth's magnetic field, it can be confused by nearby metallic or magnetic objects or electronic devices. Usually the cause is manmade: knife, belt buckle, eyeglass rims, camera or light meter, binoculars, zipper, wire fence, powerline, ice axe, steel eating utensils. If it's close enough to the compass, even an object as small as a paper clip can mess things up. Never try to use a compass inside a building, on the hood of your car, or on a picnic table.

> My snow-camping students stood patiently in a cold-footed cluster, mittened hands manipulating compasses as we practiced taking bearings to fix our location. Everyone reached close agreement except for one fellow, whose readings put us somewhere in the next county. Our search for a possible deflecting object finally unearthed the culprit: a can of foot powder buried in his front-riding beltpack.

One of the most common sources of needle deflection is another compass held too close, that is, less than several inches away. Two hikers comparing compass readings or plotting bearings on the same map may find their needles influenced by each other, so that neither gives an accurate reading.

Rarely, the compass will be thrown off by something you can't see: a local magnetic disturbance or a deposit of metallic ore. Atop a rocky outcropping near our mountain camp, friends and I found that an ore deposit was strong enough to influence our compass needles when we squatted close to the ground, but not when we stood and held our compasses just a few feet higher.

Another source of deflection sometimes occurs at high elevations: a bubble can form as the liquid in the housing contracts with changing air pressure, especially in severe cold. A bubble larger than 0.25 inch can nudge the needle and produce a false reading. Such an altitude-induced bubble will disappear when you return to a lower elevation.

When you shop for a compass, make sure that there's no bubble in the housing (this indicates a leak) and that the needle swings freely and points in the same direction as the others in the store.

Compass Directions

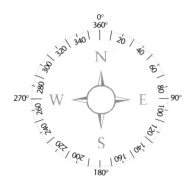

Compass directions

Remember when you learned in high-school geometry that a circle is divided into 360 degrees? Well, a compass face is simply a circle marked off in degrees by numbers from 0 to 360. Measured clockwise from the top (0 degrees, or north), a fourth of the way around the circle is an angle of 90 degrees, or east. South, being exactly a half-circle across from north, is located at 180 degrees. West is at 270 degrees. A second set of markers divides the compass face into quarters: the cardinal points N, E, S and W (north, east, south, west).

Using a Compass

First, for maximum accuracy, remember these rules:

- *Directly face* the object to which you're measuring the bearing.
- Keep the compass *level* (what would be parallel to the

floor, if the outdoors had one). Tilting it keeps the needle from swinging freely.

- Hold the compass *directly in front of you*, not at an angle.
- To align magnetic needle and orienting arrow, hold the compass close enough so that you look *down* on the face, not sideways at it. You'll be able to make the needle lie exactly straight over the orienting arrow, with their points lined up.

Setting a Bearing

To familiarize yourself with the basic uses of a compass, turn the moveable housing until N lines up with the index line. Some models are also labeled "Read bearing here." You have *set a bearing* of north, which is the same as 0 degrees or 360 degrees. After checking around for deflecting objects, hold the compass level in front of you at an easy reading distance. Now turn your body and the compass as one until the north-seeking end of the needle lines up over the pointed end of the orienting arrow. You have pointed yourself on a bearing toward magnetic north. To follow that bearing, move along the line pointed to by the direction-of-travel arrow.

Compass set for magnetic north: N *is at the index line; the red end of the magnetic needle lines up over the orienting arrow.*

(Magnetic north is different from map north or true north, but don't worry about that now; I'll explain it later. When using a compass alone—that is, without a map—as a constant directional reference, it doesn't matter that the needle points to a different north than the map does. What matters is that we can count on it to point consistently in a given direction.)

Now choose another bearing, or direction toward something, of 140 degrees. Turn the housing until 140 lines up with the index line. Turn body and compass until the north-seeking end of the needle lines up over the pointed end of the orienting arrow. The direction-of-travel arrow tells you which way to go to follow a bearing of 140 degrees.

Compass set for 140 degrees

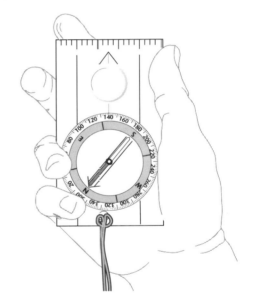

You can see that this procedure lets you pick any bearing, set it, and get yourself pointed in that direction. There will be more later about how to travel that way.

Measuring a Bearing

The next basic compass skill is to *measure a bearing (direction) to some landmark you're looking at.* This is done by simply reversing the steps.

1. Face the landmark, extend your arm and point the compass's direction-of-travel arrow at the landmark.
2. Bring the compass closer, to a good reading position, checking to make sure the travel arrow still points to the landmark.
3. Turn the housing until the pointed end of the orienting arrow lies under the north-seeking end of the needle.
4. Read the bearing at the index line. Now you know the exact direction to the landmark you chose, expressed as an angle.

These two simple procedures—setting a bearing and measuring a bearing—are basic to getting around and knowing where you are in the wild.

In measuring bearings, a factor you can't always do something about, but need to recognize, is that *the farther away the landmark, the less precise your bearing.* To illustrate: three people standing 10 yards apart in a clearing measure the bearing to a peak 40 miles away. Their answers will all agree, within a degree or two. However, if from the same positions they measure the bearing to a tree on the opposite side of the clearing, their answers will differ by many more degrees. Because of this factor, you should use short bearings when practical, and to improve precision.

Following a Bearing

You've decided on a day hike to Basket Butte, whose bare top you can see about 1 mile from camp. If you could keep the goal in sight all the way, of course, you wouldn't need any other guide. But you know Basket Butte will disappear from view when you enter the trees ahead, and when you walk through a dip in the rolling terrain. So you measure the bearing to the butte; it is 60 degrees. Now how do you use this information to get there?

With a compass, you can travel a reasonably straight line to your destination even when you lose sight of it on the way. But just heading out on the proper bearing won't keep you on the line between start and goal. In fact, you could keep the needle and orienting arrow aligned as you walk and *still* drift sideways off your line. (Try it!) The reason is that there are an infinite number of 60-degree bearings that lie parallel to each other, but only *one* connects your starting point and destination.

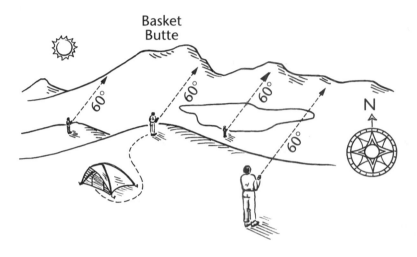

The world is full of 60-degree bearings, but only one of them connects your start and your goal.

The trick is to pick **intermediate landmarks** along the line from start to goal, traveling the distance in short legs from one landmark to the next. To do this, follow these steps:

1. Measure the bearing. Once this bearing is set, don't turn the housing at any time while you're following it.
2. Look ahead along the line of the direction-of-travel arrow and choose a landmark you can keep in sight and get to from your starting point—perhaps a distinctive snag on the far side of a huge clearing. In dense woods the best intermediate landmark might be only 50 feet away.
3. Now ignore the compass and walk to this landmark by the easiest route. Don't walk with head bent, peering at the compass and tripping over logs. As you walk, it's

the *landmark* that keeps you on course, not the alignment of needle and arrow.

4. When you get to the snag or rock, make sure you are again headed in the right direction, on your original bearing line. To do this, hold the compass in front of you—don't touch that housing!—and turn body and

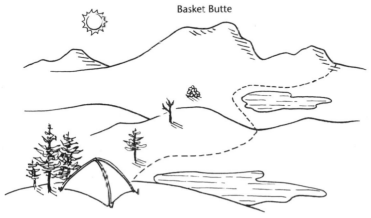

WRONG: No intermediate landmarks used

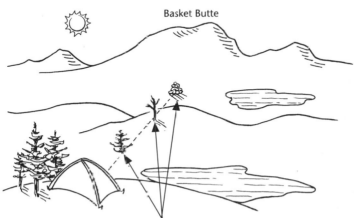

RIGHT: Using intermediate landmarks

Intermediate landmarks are checkpoints along the travel line that keep a hiker on course.

compass together until the north-seeking needle end matches the pointed end of the orienting arrow.

5. Pick another landmark along the bearing line and walk to it. Repeat this process as often as needed to cover the distance between camp and Basket Butte.

In choosing a landmark, recognize the possibility that you could lose sight of it when you hike lower than your sighting point. Also remember that it may look different when viewed from varying distances and slightly different angles.

There is another caution to observe when traveling by intermediate landmarks. It underscores the need to orient yourself with the compass *at each landmark* (step number 4, page 55) to be sure you are headed in the right direction for the next leg. Gravity is ever operative. If given a choice, the body usually wants to go the easy way: downhill. You can test this by guessing (before you check the compass) which way your travel line heads. Doing this a few times will convince you to trust compass over instincts.

There can be situations in which choosing intermediate landmarks along your travel line becomes difficult or even impossible. Perhaps on your way to Basket Butte you come to a thickly forested area where all the trees look alike. Or to another place where dozens of windfalls litter your path. On this stretch, to get to each intermediate landmark safely you must redirect your attention to climbing over or around the downed trees, so you lose track of *which* stump or tree you were heading for. Another situation might be that your line goes across a field with a berry patch in the middle. You can see a bit of field beyond, but there's nothing distinctive to aim for. Or perhaps, on another hike, you must go for help, but clouds hug the ground and you can see only 50 feet ahead.

There's a way to remain safely on your desired travel line in all these situations. Simply use your hiking partner as a **portable intermediate landmark**. Staying behind, the person with the compass (who knows where the line points) sends the other person ahead. He directs his partner with arm signals until the "landmark" is on the line and as far ahead as is safe. Then the forward person waits for the compass person to catch up, and they repeat the procedure as often as needed.

In extremely bad visibility and serious weather, the two

might rope together. In all situations, they need to stay within sight and earshot, so that the "landmark" doesn't get too far ahead. Arm signals are reliably clearer than voice commands, especially in noisy wind or rain. The following are suggested signals:

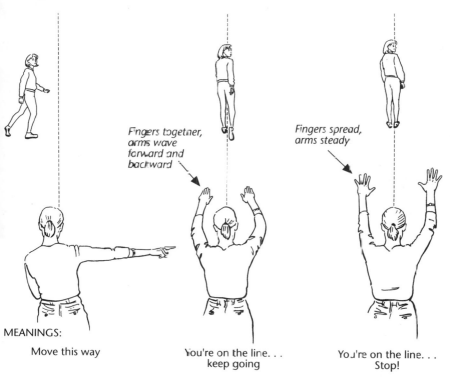

Fingers together, arms wave forward and backward

Fingers spread, arms steady

MEANINGS:

Move this way

You're on the line. . .
keep going

You're on the line. . .
Stop!

The compass holder uses arm signals to direct her partner into place as a portable intermediate landmark.

Keeping on Your Bearing by Backsighting

When traveling along a line of sight between landmarks, you may occasionally lose the one you're headed for and wonder if you're still on the right line. Or, you may get to the "distinctive" boulder you picked and discover that there's a very similar one 40 feet away. Doubt creeps in. Are you on the line? To check, sight back to the landmark you came from. Face it, compass in hand, and point the direction-of-travel arrow at the landmark. Don't turn the housing. If you're on the line, the "south" (non-colored) end of the needle will be aligned with the pointed end of the orienting arrow. If it isn't, move to one side or the other—keeping the direction-of-travel arrow pointed at the landmark—until it is.

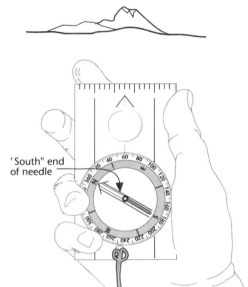

'South" end of needle

Backsighting: the travel arrow points to the object, and the non-colored end of the needle lines up with the orienting arrow.

When traveling a bearing, you can also build in the possibility of a quick backsighting check in the following way, which could sometimes be just the added safety measure needed. Before you start out, turn around and backsight along the backward extension of your travel line: keeping the bearing set, turn body and compass until the "south" end of the needle lines up with the pointed end of the orienting arrow. Look where the direction-of-travel arrow points. Is there any fairly tall feature on this line? If there is, you might later be able to backsight toward it, should you lose or lack a closer landmark.

Backbearings

During lunch atop Basket Butte you had a great view for miles around, including the tent specks of your camp on the far side of that big clearing. Now, to get back. You know that once you're off the hill, camp will be hidden from view.

In essence, your course will be the reverse of the one that

got you here, exactly opposite on the compass circle. If your original bearing was 60 degrees, the opposite number on the dial (a half-circle or 180 degrees away) would be 240 degrees (60 + 180 = 240). If the original bearing is more than 180 degrees, simply subtract the half-circle. A bearing of 300 degrees would have a backbearing of 120 degrees (300 – 180 = 120).

That's the concept. There are two ways to follow a backbearing, both easy.

- In the first method you figure the new return bearing as above and reset it on the compass, then travel by intermediate landmarks as before.

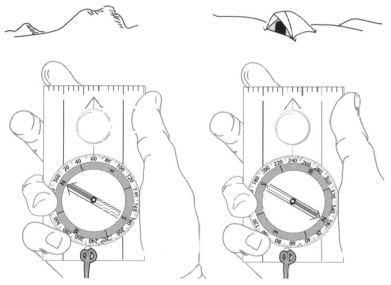

One way to return to a starting point: figure and set the backbearing, which is opposite the original bearing on the compass dial.

- In the alternate method you don't change the compass setting at all (this eliminates the possibility of making a mathematical error). Instead, hold the compass in front of you, with the original bearing still set. Now turn body and compass until the "south" end of the needle ends up with the pointed end of the orienting arrow, just as it did in backsighting. Now travel on your backbearing with this different method of needle matching, using intermediate landmarks.

In the above example your starting and ending point was clear, but in any situation where it isn't so conspicuous you should leave a visible marker at the beginning of your route. Then, if you don't hit the exact spot after traveling the right time and distance, mark where you are and search in a widening spiral for your destination point.

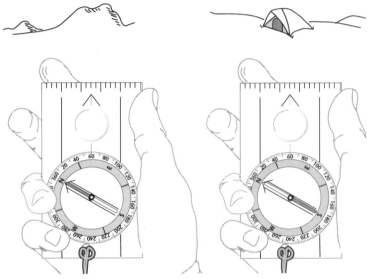

Another way to return to a starting point: keep the original bearing set, but line up the non-colored needle end with the orienting arrow.

Keeping Track of Direction

A compass kept handy as you hike can be pulled out for frequent quick checks on the direction you're traveling. Suppose that map study at home and along the way indicated that your trail heads west for the first 2 miles. Are you moving in the direction you ought to be? Point the direction-of-travel arrow ahead along the trail, and turn the housing until the arrows line up. Read the bearing at the index line. Allowing for inevitable meanderings of the trail, is the bearing somewhere in the neighborhood of 270 degrees, or west?

There may be times when trail markings or signs are unclear and you want to ease your mind about where you are. A compass check on direction can either reassure you or point out that you're probably not where you want to be.

Travel Toward a Baseline

This is one of the simplest applications of compass skills, but it could be the one that gets you found. A **baseline** is any long, fairly straight linear landmark whose direction from you is known, and that, when reached, could guide you to a desired destination or out safely.

Often your hiking territory will include a ridge, a powerline cut, the shore of a long lake, a trail, or a generally straight road or river. What's important is that you know what direction the baseline is from you, so that you can hike to it and ultimately get where you want to go.

For example, uncertain of your location, you want to head out. You know that a north–south ridgeline lies west of your hiking area and that a road crosses a pass through the ridge about 2 miles south.

Set your compass bearing for west (270 degrees) and travel to the base of the ridge, using intermediate landmarks to keep you on an efficient, direct course. When you reach the base, turn and follow it south until you intercept the road.

But what about the difference between "map north" and "compass north"? Aren't "map west" and "compass west" different, too? Yes, they are, but when used for travel toward a baseline such as this, a compass bearing of west will get you there. It's close enough.

All you need for this procedure is a general knowledge of the area that will enable you to choose a feature to use as a baseline. If you have a map, the problem is solved. It's good to figure out the baseline possibilities *before* your hike. Then, even if you lose the map, you can get found as long as you have a compass that will guide you toward the baseline.

Long, straight roads are good baselines. Rivers and big streams make unmistakable baselines, but small streams can

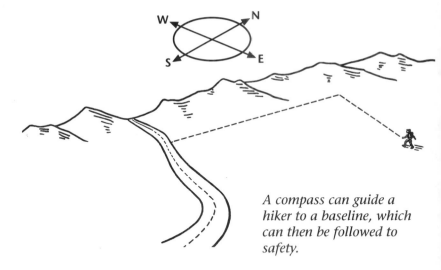

A compass can guide a hiker to a baseline, which can then be followed to safety.

be misidentified. They might also dry up. In addition, maps aren't infallible. They sometimes picture streams that aren't actually there and omit sizeable streams that clearly should be shown.

A maintained trail could be a good baseline on a summer hike but unreliable when snow-covered. A friend and I know we crossed the Pacific Crest Trail on our ski outing, because we started west of it and ended east, but we weren't aware of it when we crossed. If a trail has been abandoned or is obscured by lingering snow patches, or if it's simply too early in the season for maintenance work to have been done, a summer hiker could likewise cross a trail unknowingly. Choose your baselines carefully.

The Old 1–2–3

Here's a wilderness maneuver that makes use of three ideas we've covered:

1. Measuring the bearing to a landmark.
2. Using that bearing as a baseline when you want to make a side excursion.
3. Getting home on the backbearing of your original bearing.

From camp you sight on a notch in the ridge to the west, knowing you want to explore some small lakes that lie a bit north of that line. Think of the camp-to-notch bearing as a baseline "trail" by which you will return after your side trip to the lakes.

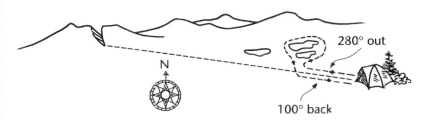

Backbearings can be used as "trails" to guide your wilderness travel.

Head out on the original bearing (280 degrees in this example) and move north "off trail" when you know you're close to the lakes. When you're ready to go back to camp, walk south to your baseline "trail." How will you know when you reach this invisible trail? Take periodic bearings on the notch as you hike south. When the bearing reads 280 degrees, you're back on the original line. Now figure the backbearing to camp (280 – 180 = 100) and travel it.

The key to this procedure is to be very careful about recording the *exact* point of the landmark you use for the sighting and to sight on that same spot later. A definite notch, for instance, is more precise than the top of a round hill.

With any route-finding procedure that's at all complex or involves more than one bearing that must be remembered, you should make notes about the important parts.

Deliberate Error

I'm not talking about getting lost on purpose, but about a special technique for avoiding that situation. When you're heading for a baseline, sometimes it's because you want to get to a certain point on that line—maybe where your car is parked on a road.

Say you hike south after leaving the car on an east–west

road. If you try to return to the car by the exact backbearing, north, the chances are pretty good you'll miss it. That's not disastrous, since you'll at least be on the road somewhere. But which way should you turn to reach the car? You'll just have to guess, and possibly waste time and energy going in the wrong direction. If you've come out to get help for an injured companion, that lost time could be crucial.

Deliberate error (also called "aiming off" or "intentional offset") makes the right guess for you. Instead of following a backbearing that you hope will lead to the point on the baseline, you can deliberately plan to hit the line to one side or the other of your destination. Then, when you reach the baseline you'll know which way to turn.

An offset of 10 degrees for a 1-mile course is reasonable; make the deviation a bit smaller as your travel distance lengthens. Deliberate error is useful in any situation where you want

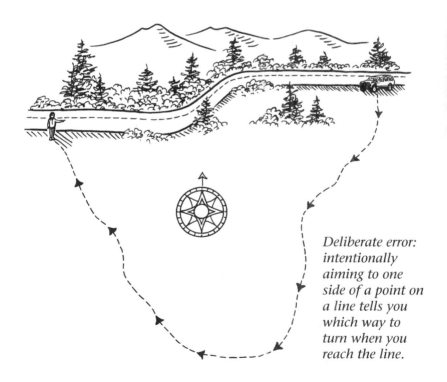

Deliberate error: intentionally aiming to one side of a point on a line tells you which way to turn when you reach the line.

to find a point on a line: a bridge over a river, your camp near the base of a long rock wall, a lake at the beginning of a stream.

Getting Around Obstacles

You're well on your way to Basket Butte. Coming over a small rise in the trees, you find a sizeable lake smack on the line of travel. It's a clear day and you can see across this barrier, but you'll have to walk off course to get around it.

There are two versions of this problem. The aim in both, of course, is to resume travel on the right line once you clear the obstacle. That seems obvious until you remember that just lining yourself up on the right bearing won't do it. Remember, along that lake shore there are a zillion parallel 60-degree bearings; you want the one that connects *your* starting point and destination.

In the simplest version, you sight across the lake and note that there's a distinctive landmark on the opposite shore exactly on your bearing line. Note carefully the point on the near shore where you head off the line, marking it in some nondestructive, temporary way if you have to: pile up some rocks, make a tripod of sticks (use downed wood; don't cut any). tie

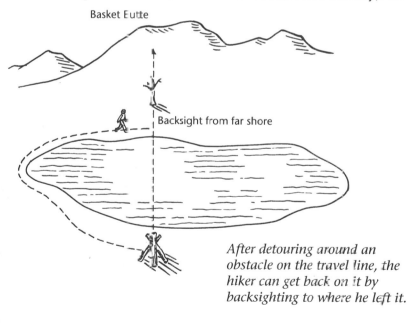

Basket Butte

Backsight from far shore

After detouring around an obstacle on the travel line, the hiker can get back on it by backsighting to where he left it.

some toilet paper securely to a branch behind you. It's a very common error to skip this step, and thus to lose your line. Now walk around to the opposite landmark. Things look different from a distance and from other angles, so if there's any doubt in your mind about being on your line, *backsight* to the point you left on the other shore. If the "south" end of the compass needle doesn't line up over the pointed end of the orienting arrow, move along the edge of the lake until it does.

In the second version of an obstacle you can see across, there is no suitable landmark on the opposite shore; the whole shoreline looks the same. If you are alone, then it is *imperative* that you find or make a landmark where you are. In addition, take one more precaution: before you leave the near shore, turn around and backsight along your travel line. Is there any feature behind you, near or far, that you might be able to backsight on once you round the lake? After you've reached the far shore, backsight toward the marker you left and move along the shore until you're on the original bearing line again. If you're hiking with a partner, send him around to the far shore, guiding him to your line with hand signals (see page 57), then catch up.

These two methods work fine if you can see around the obstacle in your path. But suppose the block is a huge, jumbled boulder pile you can't see over and certainly don't want to climb through? Or suppose a low fog hangs over the lake, obscuring the far shore? Or that clouds, rain, or snowfall limit visibility in the whole area?

Then there's only one way to get around the obstacle and have any hope of picking up your line on the other side. It involves pacing away from the course at a known angle—preferably a right angle.

Here's how. First, before you begin to maneuver around the obstacle, turn around and backsight along your travel line into the distance. There may be some feature tall enough to be seen from beyond the obstacle, once you clear it and move away from it.

Now faced with the obstacle, turn at a right angle and walk until you're past the rockpile, *counting your steps* (or paces, double steps) as you go. Write down the number. Once past the end of it, resume your original bearing and move forward again until you've cleared the obstacle. Then make a right-angle turn heading back to your original course and *go the same number of paces*. If the obstacle is very large, you measure your detour and return legs in elapsed time—write it down—rather than steps, factoring in differences in uphill and downhill travel.

The compass's rectangular base plate lets you make the right-angle turns without doing any calculations or resetting bearings; besides eliminating fuss, this rules out the possibility of mathematical errors and forgetting your original bearing. You simply sight across the *back edge* of the base plate (for a landmark to keep you on course) during the two paced legs of the detour—while keeping the needle and orienting arrow lined up—and sight normally along the direction-of-travel arrow the rest of the time. The compass remains pointed the same way relative to the obstacle throughout this maneuver, but *you* move

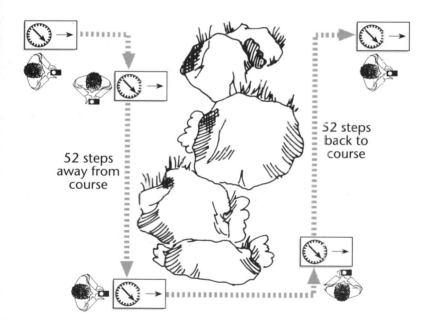

52 steps
away from
course

52 steps
back to
course

When you can't see across an obstacle, detour around it in a series of right-angle turns, then pick up the travel line.

around it. During the paced stretches the compass will be held crosswise in your hand, pointing left when you turn right and right when you turn left.

Having a mind uneasy with the simplest of spatial relationships, I find it clearest to actually walk around the unmoving compass for each change in order to point myself in the right direction. Maybe you won't need to do that. Note in the illustration the positions of hiker and compass for each leg of the detour. The compass doesn't change position, but the hiker does.

The back edge of the compass serves as a travel arrow on the legs away from and back to your original travel line.

Another thing that helps when you need to do a route-finding procedure such as this one, is to draw a simple map of what you're doing, writing down the number of steps on the detour and return legs. A sketch is particularly helpful should the maneuver turn out to be more complicated than you anticipate, as in the following situation:

You are working your way around a fog-shrouded lake and think you've cleared the end after the second turn, only to find that an arm of the lake juts out to block your way. You must throw in another set of turns to get around the arm.

If this happens on the leg where you don't count steps, as in example A, make another right-angle turn away from the obstacle and go as far as you must to clear the finger, *counting steps as you do so.* Add this number to the number of steps in your first detour leg. Write it down. Now resume forward travel on the original bearing until, when you look over your shoulder, the way is clear. Now make a right-angle turn heading back toward your original course and go the *total* number of paces.

If the unexpected finger of the obstacle occurs on the return leg, say when you've gone 30 steps as in example B, write this number down. Then make another right-angle turn. Go as far as you must to clear the finger when you look over your shoulder. Now make a right-angle turn heading back to your original course and go the other 22 steps needed to equal the first detour leg.

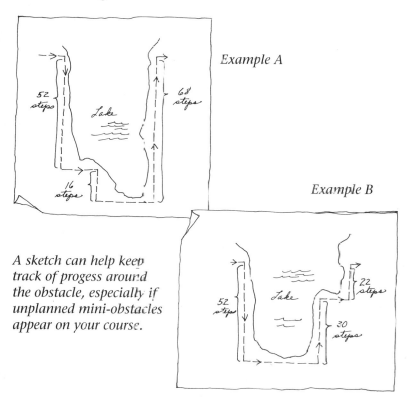

Example A

Example B

A sketch can help keep track of progess around the obstacle, especially if unplanned mini-obstacles appear on your course.

Relocating a Place

When Sam and Sal ventured down a barely discernible overgrown trail, they found a delightful meadow. They definitely wanted to be able to find this special place again, but since the takeoff point from the main trail was so unclear, they took steps to fix the junction's location in their memories. Physically marking the spot would undoubtedly lead others to their private discovery. Instead, Sam and Sal marked it another way.

Back at the junction, they searched the surrounding terrain for a prominent landmark and took a bearing on it, then made a note: "Junction to our meadow: go west on Tamarack Trail until the north end of the bald ridge is at 72 degrees." To make the hiking a bit easier, they might also have noted the bearing on which the overgrown trail starts off: "Trail starts through the larches at 118 degrees."

I've used this technique frequently in areas that I first hike in summer and to which I want to return on skis in winter months. With several feet of snow cover, even major trails are often elusive. The only modification I make then in the basic procedure is to use a fairly close landmark for the crucial bearing, since poor winter visibility is likely to limit my viewing range.

This basic procedure of traveling on a known line until you reach a spot marked by one bearing is a variant on the baseline method and is useful in many different situations. You might want to hike along a ridgeline until you reach a draw that leads to a good beaver pond at the base of the hill. But the ridge overlooks many draws, so you should "mark" the one you want with a bearing from that spot to some prominent feature.

On another hike you follow a stream about 1 mile and discover some interesting caves out of sight up the east bank. Go back to where you left the stream and get a bearing on some landmark you'd be sure to see when you come back again, perhaps some lichen-covered crags upstream. On return trips to areas such as this, travel the baseline stream until you reach

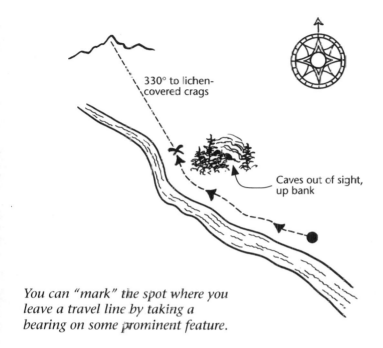

330° to lichen-covered crags

Caves out of sight, up bank

You can "mark" the spot where you leave a travel line by taking a bearing on some prominent feature.

the particular spot "marked" by the crossbearing to the chosen landmark.

A step beyond this method for relocating a spot is when you must use *two* bearings: one for the first line of travel (the baseline) and the second to find the spot on that line. You could use this method to find a cached food supply, the area of a big lake where the fishing was terrific, or a can of water you stashed for a desert hike.

When you bury the water supply, mark it and take a bearing back to a landmark along the approach line of your future hike. Choose something prominent and permanent so you can count on finding it later. Write this bearing down: "Cache about ten minutes' walk from south end of layered cliff face, bearing 210 degrees." Now look for a second landmark, preferably close to 90 degrees away from the first; this will give you a more accurate fix than if you use landmarks too close together or too far apart. Twin buttes rise off to the east a bit, so you note the facts: "Saddle between buttes, 138 degrees."

On the return trip, you reach the first landmark, the south end of the layered cliff face. To head on the line that will lead to your cache, check the bearing in your notes. Because you're now hiking the *backbearing* of that, subtract 180 from the original 210, and head out on 30 degrees. When you've walked for almost ten minutes, begin taking trial bearings on the saddle between the twin buttes. Be sure to *stay on* your first travel line as you do so. When the bearing to the saddle reads 138 degrees, you should be very near your cache.

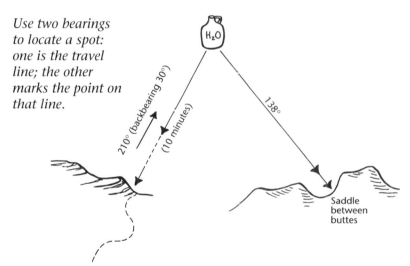

Use two bearings to locate a spot: one is the travel line; the other marks the point on that line.

Another, very important, application of this technique for relocating a spot described by the intersection of two bearings would be to bring rescuers to an injured companion. Actually working your way back to a spot is difficult, particularly in poor visibility and rough country, and over long distances. But if you doubt your own ability to return, you could still give rescuers the information so *they* could do it. A key thing to tell them is that the bearings you give are *magnetic* bearings (rather than "true bearings").

Before you leave your friend, measure at least two bearings to features that could likely be seen from a couple of miles away. As a safety precaution, take two or three extra bearings on features at varying distances from the spot. Also note distinctive objects nearby: a snag that could be seen as one approached, a lone pine on a crag just to the west. *Write all this information down.* Draw a rough sketch if you feel it will help you remember details.

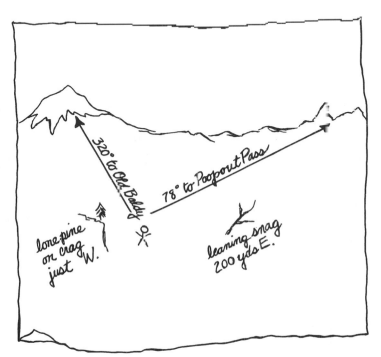

A sketch of where you've left an injured friend will guide you back with help. Note at least two bearings, as well as prominent nearby features.

When you've hiked out and are ready to go back with help, it's unlikely that you'll be starting exactly on one of your two key bearings (as you were in the water cache problem). First travel in the general direction until you can see one of the features you used, then begin taking trial bearings on it. When the bearing matches the original one (320 degrees to Old Baldy, in the illustration above), travel on that line until you spot the second feature.

Now comes the tricky part. *Remain on the first line* while taking periodic bearings on the second feature. When this second bearing matches your original bearing (78 degrees to Poopout Pass, in the illustration), you are very near your waiting friend. Begin to shout and blow your whistle, and look for the nearby features you noted in your description.

How Important Is Accuracy in Compass Use?

Using a hiker's compass is not an exactly perfect operation. Depending on the distance traveled, you might be from several yards to a small fraction of a mile off your goal. (Then you bring into play your map-reading skills and all the staying-found behaviors discussed in Chapters 9 and 10.) But when care is taken at every step of measuring and following bearings, the result is certainly precise enough for wilderness travel.

This formula may convince you of the need for being thorough and careful: for every degree of error, a hiker will be 88 feet off target in 1 mile of travel. So if a bearing is wrong by 6 degrees and a hiker travels 4 miles, the goal would be missed by 0.4 mile.

Walking in the Real World

You'll note that, as shown in the illustration, the hiker's path isn't straight. The hiker isn't drunk or daydreaming but does make inevitable small detours in following a general bearing—around the end of a big log in the way, skirting a rise instead of going over the top, avoiding a squishy low spot.

Actual hiking can rarely be done in a straight line, since land has so many irregularities. The idea is to be conscious of the deviations you make off your course, keep them short, and try to zig as often as you zag. If you must make a sizeable move, however, you're better off plotting a new travel bearing.

Given the necessity of occasional detours and the fact that a compass isn't perfectly precise, you may be surprised at how close you can usually come to your destination. Moreover, you can improve the odds when you do any of the following:

- Make careful, accurate sightings on both destination and intermediate landmarks.

- Follow the direction-of-travel arrow, not the compass needle, when walking a bearing.
- Recheck bearings carefully to avoid an accumulation of small errors.
- Use bearings over *short* distances when possible.
- Aim for a line rather than a point, when feasible; for instance, a stream is easier to hit than a waterfall on that stream.
- Line up two distant objects on your bearing line that will always be in sight—for example, a prominent tree and a crag. When you have to detour off course, quickly correct for error by moving until these points are again aligned.
- Continually relate your progress to the map.

Straight-line travel is rare in the wilds; keep track of your off-course deviations.

Putting Map and Compass Together

Using a map with a compass is easy when you hike near a fairly straight line that runs through western Florida, middle Tennessee, near Chicago, across western Lake Superior, and near the western edge of Hudson Bay. Along that line a compass needle points toward the geographic north pole, **true north**, the direction most maps call north.

Elsewhere it's not quite as simple, and most North American hikers find that their compass needles point either a bit east or west of true north. The needle doesn't really point *to* anything, but it tries to line up with the earth's magnetic field. Greatly simplifying, we say that these irregular magnetic lines meet at the magnetic north and south poles, and that a compass needle points to one of the two slowly changing areas. The 1992 location of the north magnetic polar region was about 950 miles from the geographic north pole, in the Sverdrup Islands of the Canadian Arctic.

Actually, in large areas of the world a compass needle may point ten degrees or more *away* from the direction of the magnetic pole. No matter. What's important to a foot traveler is a clear understanding that the compass needle doesn't point to true north.

The difference between true north and where your compass needle points is called **magnetic declination**. Because the magnetic polar regions move, this difference varies from place to place and changes very slowly from year to year. In order to use a map and compass together you need to know the declination for your hiking area. All good topographic maps will give this information for the year the map was issued. On older USGS maps there's an angle diagram in the lower left margin showing the relative positions of true and magnetic north and the declination in degrees.

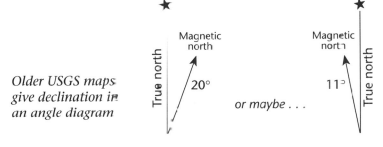

Older USGS maps give declination in an angle diagram

Newer USGS maps give declination in the lower left corner in degrees and minutes, omitting the angle diagram. Privately produced and Forest Service maps usually include declination in their legends.

A caution is in order about declination diagrams: they give the *direction* of declination, but not necessarily the correct *size*. Especially for small declinations, the size may be exaggerated. *Get the size from the printed number.*

In North America this declination can be anything from zero to 34 degrees east (in Kaktovik, Alaska). Hikers in northern Maine have a westerly declination of 20 degrees. As we noted, some lucky folks travel along a line where the declination is zero degrees. This is called the *agonic* line; the others are *isogonic* lines. Those of us with anything other than a zero-degree declination must make an adjustment when we use a map—which is laid out along *true* north–south lines—with a compass.

Lest you be tempted to ignore the declination and hope it won't matter, consider these consequences. For *each* degree ignored, you'll be off one-sixtieth of whatever distance you travel. Translated, that's 88 feet per degree in 1 mile of walking. Multiply that 88 feet by your declination, and you could be lost. A hiker in northern Maine (declination 20 degrees west) traveling to a lake 1 mile away would end up a third of a mile from goal. In eastern New Mexico (declination 10 degrees east) the error would be a sixth of a mile in 1 mile of travel, still enough to confuse a person pretty thoroughly. The farther one travels, the larger the error. So if the New Mexico hiker went 6 miles, he or she would be a whole mile off goal.

The earth's magnetic field is irregular, and the lines along which declination is the same are not neatly parallel. Hence declination sometimes changes abruptly and in strange patterns over the earth's surface. The 20-degrees-east declination line, for example, flows like a huge winding river over the world, but the declination is the same at all points it touches.

Declination lines indicate only the approximate declination for any point they touch (actually an average for that area). The compass needle *doesn't* point in the direction of the lines.

Fortunately, declination is fairly constant in a given area from one mile to the next. Irregularities in the earth's magnetic field create spotty declination anomalies, but odds are you could roam a lifetime and never encounter one. Daily and even seasonal variations in declination are so small that a hiker's compass won't register the changes. Therefore, once you've determined the declination for the territory you're exploring, adjust for it and trust the compass over your instincts about direction.

One more caution. The declination printed on a map was accurate for the year the map was published, yet may be a bit unreliable if many years have elapsed. Declination changes slowly, and at unpredictably varying rates over the earth. In some places in certain years there's no annual change—as in 1985 along a line through northern Maine and parts of Quebec. Yet in other areas of North America the declination may increase or decrease almost 9' (close to ⅙ of a degree) in a year. That may not sound like much, considering that a hiker's compass work isn't perfectly exact. But the USGS topographic map for an area may be thirty years old, and it's possible to have a change of 5 degrees in that period.

There are two ways you can update an outdated declina-

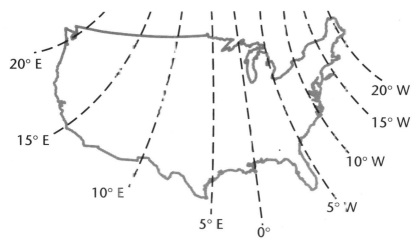

Magnetic declination in the conterminous United States, 1993

tion. One is to call the USGS (National Earthquake Information Center) at 303-273-8488. Another is to spend $6.20 on a fascinating chart available from the USGS: The Magnetic Field of the United States, Declination Chart, Map GP-986-D. This 1985 chart, usually updated every ten years, can be ordered from the address on page 35. It has two grids of lines: red lines at 1-degree intervals (every fifth one darker) show the declinations all over the country; blue lines at half-minute intervals (every tenth one darker) show the size and direction of annual change. By locating your hiking area on the chart, you can update the declinations on your old maps (note to the nearest half-degree) and the result will be a more accurate use of your map and compass.

Here's an example of how to update from the chart:

> You plan to hike in an area several miles east of Yellowstone National Park in Wyoming. The chart shows the 1985 declination (nearest red line) as 15°E and the change (nearest blue line) as 6'w. In eight years the change has been 48', ⅘ of a degree. Is this an *increase* or *decrease*? The rule is this: if declination and change are both E or w, you *add* the change. If one is E and the other w, *subtract* the change. So, subtracting the change, you'll update your declination to just over 14°E

United States declination chart, 1985

Canada's Magnetic Declination Chart 1990 (Sheet #10, $5.20 including postage) may be purchased from the following:
Geological Survey of Canada
Publications Office
601 Booth Street
Ottawa, Ontario
Canada K1A 0E9

When Does Declination Matter?

If you are using a compass alone as a constant directional reference, in the ways described in Chapter 4, "Compass," you don't need to think about the relationship between your compass directions and true north.

When you use map and compass together, however, you need to adjust for the declination. (Another situation arises when you are using your compass to measure things in relation to the sun, which, like a map, works with reference to true north. "True Directions" and "Looking to Nature" will guide you through these procedures.)

Adjusting for Declination

Always orient map and compass together as the first step in any procedure. Essentially, orienting the map with the compass adjusts for declination once and for all. You can make the correction accurately and then forget about it. And you can accomplish this matching of map and real world even if you don't know any landmarks or can't see through the fog beyond the tent door.

Here's what you do. Spread your map out *on the levelest place you can find*, lining it up approximately with the landscape if you can see. (A tip for orienting the map when the ground is wet: first lay down a piece of lightweight plastic the size of your map.) Check around for metal or electronic objects that could confuse the compass needle. Now turn the compass housing so that N is exactly at the index line. With N

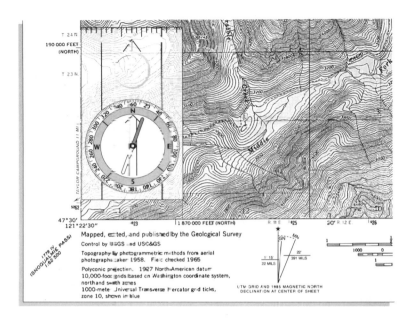

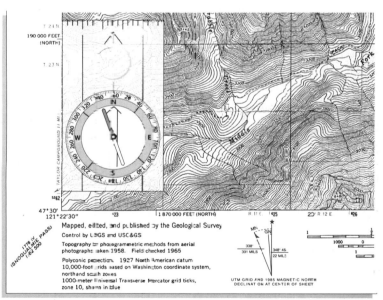

*Map oriented with compass: **top**, easterly declination; **bottom**, westerly declination.*

toward the top of the map, place one side edge of the base plate along either side edge of the map (the *only* lines guaranteed by the mapmakers to run true north–south).

Holding the map and compass in this position, carefully turn them together to achieve the following:

1. **For an easterly declination:** the north-seeking end of the needle points to the number on the dial that is your declination (or aligns with the declination tape if you've added one).
2. **For a westerly declination:** the needle points to 360 minus the declination (or aligns with the declination tape if you've added one).

The map is now "oriented." Directions on the map match directions on the land around you. *Anchor the edges of the map* with rocks, sticks, or any nonmetal gear. **It's *very* important that the map remain oriented during all map and compass procedures.** Once the map is in this position, don't move it!

Where Are We, Anyhow?

In the city, you can determine or describe your location by referring to the intersection of the street you're on and the nearest cross-street. In the wild, the same idea—locating yourself by the intersection of lines—can show you approximately where you are.

If you know you are somewhere along a line—a trail, ridge, stream—then you already have one line and need only one more in order to find your location on the map. If you aren't on a known line, you need at least *two* lines, and, for a more precise fix, three.

To get the lines you need, take bearings on identifiable landmarks. When these bearings are plotted on the map their intersecting lines mark where you are. This procedure is called **triangulation** and **crossbearings**.

Here's how to do it. First, orient and anchor your map. Look around for a landmark some distance away that you can identify on the map and take a bearing on it: point the direction-of-travel arrow at a particular part of the landmark—not just a hill, but the highest part; not just a cliff face, but its north end. Turn the housing until the pointed end of the orienting arrow lies under the north-seeking end of the needle. The bearing from you to the landmark can be read at the index line, but you don't really need to know what it is in order to plot it on the map. Just don't turn the housing once the bearing has been taken.

Now place the compass on the oriented map with one *front* base-plate corner right on the symbol for the landmark, being sure to use the part of the feature you took the bearing on. *Don't move the map.* Keeping this corner in place as a pivot, rotate the whole compass, base plate and all, until the pointed end of the orienting arrow and the needle are again lined up. You have recreated on the map the line you measured in the air.

Starting at the pivot corner, draw a line along the base-plate edge (mark the line with a folded piece of paper if you don't have a pencil). If you already know you are on a given line, this landmark bearing will cross the line at your approximate location. Often it's enough just to note where the line goes; you won't need to actually draw it on the map.

If you had no idea about your position, the landmark bearing tells you that you are *somewhere* along the bearing line. To find out where, take a bearing on a second known landmark and plot it on the map in the same way. You may need to extend the lines until they cross. A folded piece of paper such as another map works well, overlapped with the compass base plate a couple of inches to ensure against skewing the line. The intersection of the extended lines marks your location. If the lines don't cross, you probably plotted one or both in the opposite direction from the landmark.

A third bearing will produce an even better fix. The most accurate results will come from using bearings close to 90 degrees apart, which isn't always possible. If bearings are either very close together or close to a half-circle apart, the intersection won't be as precise.

If you start out knowing nothing about where you are except that you can identify one landmark, don't despair. When you plot the bearing to it on the map, you at least know that you are somewhere along that line. By comparing the terrain to the map, you may be able to identify a second point of

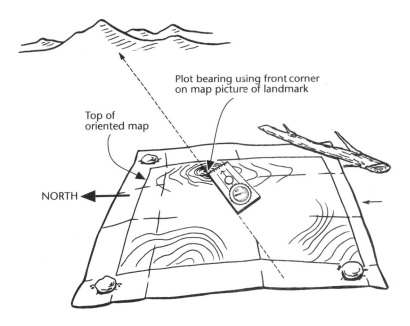

Plot bearing using front corner on map picture of landmark

Top of oriented map

NORTH

When you begin to wonder where you are, plot a bearing to a known landmark on the oriented map. You are somewhere on that line!

reference. Sometimes you can even figure out exactly *where* along the line you are.

If the location you plot by triangulation doesn't make sense with what you see around you, it may be for one of the following reasons:

- You read the compass wrong.
- You misidentified points you took bearings on.
- You incorrectly transferred bearings to the map.
- The map moved out of its oriented position.

What Are We Looking At?

If you know where you are, you can identify any visible terrain feature, provided that it's on the map. If necessary, figure your location first by triangulation.

Take a bearing on the mystery landmark and plot it *from* your spot on the oriented map *toward* the landmark. Put one *back* corner of the base plate on your location and pivot the whole compass until the needle and the pointed end of the orienting arrow line up. Starting at the pivot corner, draw a line across the map along the edge of the base plate and study the features it intersects. One of them will be your landmark.

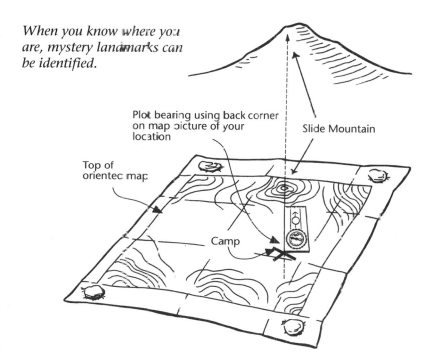

When you know where you are, mystery landmarks can be identified.

Plot bearing using back corner on map picture of your location

Slide Mountain

Top of oriented map

Camp

How can you remember whether to use a front or back corner of the compass base plate when you plot a bearing on the map? Use this simple formula: you are at the back of the compass *and* what you're looking at is at the front. *So, when you know only where you are, use a back corner; when you know only what you're looking at, use a front corner.*

Which Is Mount Challenge?

What if you want to locate one particular peak, say Mount Challenge? Orient the map. Draw (or simply lay a straightedge along) a line connecting where you are with Mount Challenge. Now place the compass so one side edge is on this line, with the direction-of-travel arrow pointing toward the peak. Turn the housing until the needle and the pointed end of the orienting arrow line up. The bearing is at the index line. Now hold the compass, making sure the needle and arrow are still aligned. The direction-of-travel arrow points to Mount Challenge.

Going Somewhere You Can't See

You might want to travel to an unseen destination for the fun and adventure of it. Perhaps you'd like to spend a day exploring a lake that lies beyond the next group of low hills, or maybe you want to plot the route for a week-long cross-country ramble. The same map-and-compass skills applied in these activities can also be used in a genuine pinch, such as going for help when visibility is poor. These are the steps to follow:

1. Orient the map.
2. Mark your start and destination.
3. Choose the best route between them.
4. Measure the route bearings on the map.
5. Follow them.

Study the map to decide on the best route for getting to your destination. The route should be energy efficient and avoid major hazards. Now, on the oriented map measure the bearings along the course you choose.

Here's how. Draw a line between your start and goal. Place the compass on the oriented map so that one side edge is on this line, with the direction-of-travel arrow pointing toward the goal. Hold the base plate steady on the line and turn the housing until the needle and pointed end of the orienting arrow line up. Read the bearing at the index line (120 degrees in the illustration of a bearing from Demaris Lake to Red Meadow).

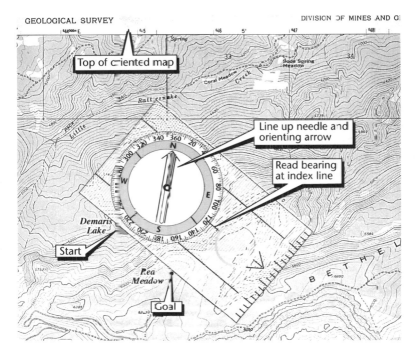

Measure a travel bearing on a map by placing the compass base plate so it touches both the start and the goal.

How do you get headed in the right direction? Load your pack, and fold the map with your travel area out for ready reference. Hold the compass horizontally in front of you with the first route bearing set, and turn yourself and the compass until the needle and the pointed end of the orienting arrow line up. Now you are pointed toward your destination—or the first leg of the route, if it consists of more than one bearing. You can now reach your goal by using the compass to get to intermediate landmarks along the way.

When your route involves more than one leg, you need to think in advance about the change from one leg to the next. How will you recognize these points, which are called **catching features**? Study the map. How far will you follow your first bearing before it hits the stream you've decided to follow for 1 mile? Given what the map says about the terrain, how long should that take? How will you know when you've followed the stream for 1 mile, at which point you plan to climb up to the nearby ridge? Perhaps a side stream comes in from the right just before this point, or perhaps the woods give way to a sizeable open stretch. If the route you've laid out calls for walking the ridge some distance before dropping over to the other side, how will you know when you've gone far enough? One way is to study the map for landmarks you should be able to see from that point, and marking and measuring the bearings on the oriented map.

Occasionally you may find it necessary to hike in very bad visibility. There should be an absolutely compelling reason, for otherwise it's safest to wait for better conditions. Suppose you hiked cross-country over a notch in a ridge yesterday, making camp in a fine valley. This morning your friend took a bad fall on slippery rocks. Assessing the situation, you decide to go for help. The ridge is rugged, but you know the notch affords a good way over, and you could be back with help in a few hours... *if* you knew where the notch was. A thick fog covers everything above the valley floor.

Fortunately, a compass works regardless of visibility, and can help you out of this predicament. Orient the map, measure the bearing from camp to notch on the map, and follow it by choosing intermediate landmarks that you can see. If available, use a partner as a portable intermediate landmark (see page 56). Write down the original bearing so you can use the backbearing to get from notch to camp in case the fog is still heavy when you return. Even if each leg of the trip is only 60 feet long, this method of travel is much wiser than wandering totally disoriented in whiteout weather.

Baselines and Deliberate Error

The idea of hiking toward a baseline works with just a compass and general knowledge of the area, but the possibilities are even broader with the added help of a map.

With map and compass you can travel toward a baseline you can't see to take a bearing on, because you can "see" the road or river on the map and accurately measure its direction from you. If you had to, you could travel on this bearing even in poor visibility.

The procedure of using deliberate error can be done better with a map than with compass alone; a map will provide a clearer idea of the destination and what sort of country you'll have to go through to reach the baseline. You can use this idea to advantage in some off-trail ramblings, too. For instance: the map shows an intriguing small lake a couple of miles from base camp. The lake has an outlet stream that you can trace on the map for a considerable distance. If you set a course for the

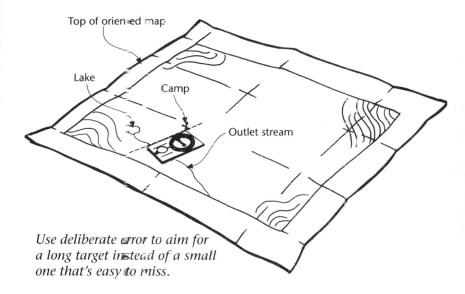

Use deliberate error to aim for a long target instead of a small one that's easy to miss.

lake itself, you would be mighty lucky to hit it exactly after a 2-mile walk, and you could miss in the direction opposite the outlet. To be sure of ultimately finding the lake, aim instead for the creek, slightly downstream from the lake.

Use this same method to return to camp near a baseline stream. Deliberately plan to hit it upstream from camp; then you'll know to travel downstream.

Bearings as Baselines

In places where a natural baseline does not exist, you can create an abstract baseline with a compass bearing measured from your starting point to some landmark—for instance, a distant peak. Another bearing to a second landmark fixes the point's exact location on the first bearing baseline.

With the crossbearings *written down* you're free to wander around the area as long as visibility allows for sighting on the landmarks you chose. As always, keep an alert eye out for weather changes.

Say your explorations take you considerably east and south of camp. Sight on the first landmark peak. Your bearing of 354

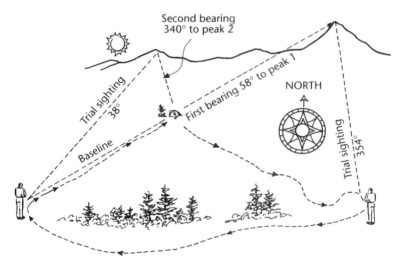

Bearings can serve as baselines that let you explore a trailless area.

degrees is way off the 58-degree reading you want, and it tells you the desired baseline is much farther west. Start sighting again when you've moved some distance to the west; your bearing will read 58 degrees as soon as you've reached the line.

Which way to turn? Sight on the second landmark. A trial bearing of 38 degrees says it was taken from west of the peak, but the 340-degree bearing from camp was taken from east of it. This tells you which way to walk along the baseline (a right turn here). The second peak will eventually be on a bearing of 340 degrees, and if you haven't strayed off the first bearing baseline, you should be very close to camp.

To avoid getting off course, remember to make use of intermediate landmarks along the bearing line, keep close track of deviations as you make them, and correct for any detours as soon as possible.

Bracketing

Bracketing is another baseline safety measure. When planning to return to a baseline, you should do everything you can to ensure that you'll be able to reach the particular *point* on that line you want. Bracketing that point with landmarks on either side is sometimes the best way. You "mark" these enclosing points far enough apart on the baseline so you'll be sure to reach it somewhere between them.

The brackets might be natural features along the line that you note from studying the map: "Camp lies at the base of the ridge, halfway between a notch to the north and the only treed gully to the south." Visible from a distance, brackets such as these make travel much easier and looser. There's no need to use compass bearings when you can sight the brackets frequently enough to keep headed in the right general direction. Keep in mind, though, that terrain features can sometimes disappear for a while, and that they might appear changed when viewed from different directions.

When your baseline is a stream, note distinctive features a distance upstream and downstream from camp: "Twin waterfalls a quarter mile upstream, narrow cliff-lined gorge half a mile downstream."

For markers you might tie paper strips to trees along the logging road where you left your car, or along the shore of a long lake, 0.5 mile or less each way from your destination. Markers of this kind should include notes about the direction of your goal, or you can make entries in your notebook when you place them: "Marker south from camp is on lone ponderosa; north marker on lodgepole pine." Remove your markers after use.

Learning These Procedures

You can practice some basic map and compass operations even at home. It's best to do this outside, away from the compass-deflecting influence of nails, pipes, and such that abound in buildings. Orient several maps of different declination until this fundamental process is automatic. Measure the bearings between a pair of points on an oriented map, and plot the best route by studying what the map indicates about the terrain along the bearing line. When you've run through this procedure several times, the different steps will begin to come easily.

Take map, compass, and this book on a hike over familiar ground in clear weather. Take bearings on landmarks you know, then plot them on the oriented map. Move to another spot, orient the map again, measure and plot more bearings. Identify a mystery feature or two. By the time you head home, you'll be friends with these routines.

When you have these basic procedures well in hand, try them in off-trail travel, nearby and in familiar territory. Measure the bearing on the oriented map to an easy off-trail goal—maybe a lake at the base of a cliff you can see from the trail, or a ridgeline pass that will offer a great lunchtime view. Carefully write down all the route-related clues you've discovered, in addition to the bearing, and go!

True Directions

There are a few instances when it's helpful to be able to measure and follow a **true direction**, a bearing measured using true north (remember, maps are laid out with the side edges running true north and south). If you want to know, for instance, which way is true east (90 degrees), a 90-degree bearing measured from magnetic north on the compass won't tell you. It would be off by the amount of your declination. Only if you were hiking somewhere along the line of zero-degree declination would true north and compass north be the same.

Measuring bearings that have to do with the sun calls for true directions also. The sun moves in relation to true directions; true north represents the endpoint of the axis on which the earth rotates. If you want to know where the sun will rise, you need to think in *true* directions because that's how the sun "thinks."

It's a fairly simple matter to adjust for this peculiarity and determine true directions. First, you need to know the magnetic declination for your hiking area. You'll find it at the bottom of the USGS topographic map, or in the legends of other maps.

To Find True North

Turn the compass housing so that N lines up with the index line. Hold the compass horizontally in front of you and turn your body and the compass as a unit until the north-seeking end of the needle points to your declination (or the declination tape, if you've added one; see page 49). For areas with an easterly declination, that will be the number itself.

A westerly declination will be found left of N, so you must subtract its number from 360 degrees, which of course is the same as N. For instance, a hiker whose declination is 16 degrees west will turn until the compass needle lines up with 344 (360 − 16).

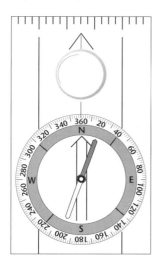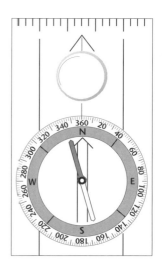

Compass oriented to true north: **left,** *in an area with a delination of 20 degrees east;* **right,** *in an area with a declination of 16 degrees west.*

You have now marked off the declination: the direction-of-travel arrow and N on the dial point to true north. You have oriented yourself so that N, E, S, and W on the compass match true north, east, south, and west in the actual landscape.

Following Other True Directions

Suppose a friend has told you about a good trail that is 0.25 mile true east of your camp. How do you get pointed in that direction? Turn the compass housing so that E (90 degrees) is at the index line. Hold the compass horizontally in front of you and turn body and compass until the north-seeking end of the needle lines up with your declination. For the declinations in the previous examples, the compass will look like this:

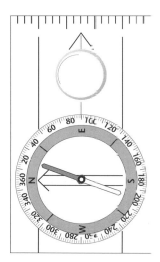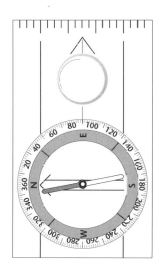

Compass set for due east: **left,** *20 degrees east;* **right,** *16 degrees west.*

To head true east, follow the direction-of-travel arrow using landmarks along your destination line.

This procedure can be used to get yourself headed on any true bearing:

1. Turn the compass housing so the number of your chosen bearing lies at the index line.
2. Turn body and compass as a unit until the north-seeking end of the needle lines up with your declination (or declination tape).
3. The direction-of-travel arrow now points along your chosen bearing.

It is helpful to have a clear picture in your mind of the relationship between true and magnetic directions, so that you can quickly convert one to the other if you wish to, without orienting the map. Say a glance at the map tells you that a peak you want to explore lies directly east of your present position, that is, on a true bearing of 90 degrees. To quickly get your travel bearing, convert this true bearing to a magnetic one by following this rule: *subtract* an east declination, *add* a west declination.

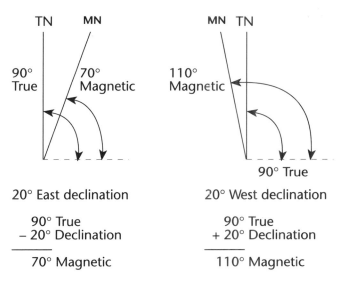

Quick conversion of true bearings to a magnetic bearings

The next chapter deals with some of the time and direction clues we can get by observing the sun. Some of the procedures involve measuring true directions and will give you a very practical way to use the skill you just learned.

Looking to Nature

So far we've been considering how to get around in the quiet places by using manmade tools: map and compass. But nature itself provides information to help us make our way. While nature's clues can give very rough ideas about direction and time, they are better than no ideas in a pinch when you lack more accurate aids. And even if no genuine emergency arises, it's fun to practice these skills and comforting to know you can estimate direction based on where the sun should be at a given time of year or on recognizable star patterns, and figure out the time of day from the sun's position.

Two basic kinds of information are constantly needed in making route-finding decisions: **direction** and **time**. The reasons for needing direction are obvious, but many people, accustomed to being able to extend daylight by a flip of a switch, underestimate the importance of time in planning their travels.

The length of day is crucial when your activities are tied to sun time. Will you reach that off-trail goal before dark? How many miles can you realistically plan to cover on a late fall hike when the sun may be setting as early as six o'clock? And sunset, if you're deep in a canyon, will come much earlier for you than for the rim walker.

This section will cover several procedures for arriving at rough estimates of direction and time by observing natural elements. Should you need to make your way using *only* information gained in this fashion, accept that your travel paths must be conservatively chosen and will lack the precision of compass routes. Without a compass you can't take bearings and travel to unseen goals by using intermediate landmarks.

What *can* you do with clues about direction and time gained from nature? Aside from the fun and satisfaction of adding this source of information to your other sources, could you really make use of it in an emergency? Yes, as long as visibility is good enough to make sun clues available. Even on an overcast day when you can't pinpoint the sun's position, a stick, ski pole, or knifeblade will often cast a faint shadow on a light surface such as paper or snow. Of course, in really poor visibility it's usually wisest to sit tight and await improved conditions or rescue.

Knowing what time it is without a watch (many people deliberately avoid using one, or you may lose or break yours) can help you judge whether to keep traveling, how far you can get, when it's time to stop and make camp, or how much exploring time is left before you need to return to base camp.

What about direction? If your compass is lost or broken, how can you stay or get found?

From your knowledge of the area and your approximate location, decide which general direction is the best way out. A map simplifies this decision, but even if you don't have one there's quite a bit of information you probably *do* have:

- how far you've traveled
- what direction you came from
- baselines in the area
- the general location of terrain to *avoid*, such as cliff systems, uncrossable streams, deep canyons, rugged mountains

In the following problems, **knowing where the sun should be** makes it possible to use it as a guide for travel. Sometimes this is as simple as walking straight toward the sun, or always keeping it to one side of your travel line. In deciding where to move in relationship to the sun, you might want to draw a rough map or diagram that makes your situation easier to visualize.

Problem 1. I hiked cross-country about 3 miles south from an east–west baseline road, and now I need to return, but without the help of the compass I lost. It's midmorning in late August, so the sun should be southeast of me in the morning and southwest in the afternoon (the sun's seasonal paths will be described later). To hike out north in the morning, I can aim generally opposite the sun and somewhat to the right, keeping it behind my *right* shoulder. When the sun is highest in the sky, my shadow will fall north. At that time I can try to spot some large landmarks to the north that provide additional guidance. If I haven't reached the baseline by the time the sun starts dropping from its highest position, then I should move along so that the sun is to the *left* and behind as the afternoon progresses. This will keep me headed generally north.

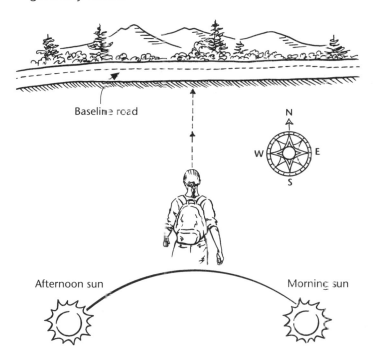

Baseline road

N
W   E
S

Afternoon sun   Morning sun

A late-summer hiker uses the sun to guide her north to a baseline road.

Problem 2. On a late December snowshoe trip I need to make my way out without a compass. There's a baseline ridge running north–south about 1 mile to the west. If I can get to the base of the ridge, I can follow it south to a highway. So I want to head west. In late December the sun's daily path is far to the southeast–southwest. It's afternoon, but with over two hours of daylight left it's reasonable to try for the ridge base. My line of travel should keep the sun in the area *between straight ahead and my left shoulder.*

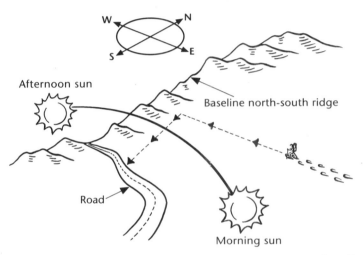

A midwinter traveler uses the sun to guide him west to a baseline he can safely follow out.

The Sun, Direction, and Time

Try to fix in your mind the sun's approximate path and its relative location from you at different times of the year. At home in the city, notice its rising and setting places as the months pass, and the changing amounts of sunlight that come through your windows at different seasons. This will keep you aware of the sun's motions during your city-bound times and reinforce the habit of noticing its location.

In the northern hemisphere the sun's path is generally south of us during fall, winter, and spring. In summer the arc will be northeast to northwest.

Only twice each year does the sun cross the equator, making day and night of approximately equal length. These times—the equinoxes—occur about March 21 and September 22. Moving gradually northward from its spring equinox position, the sun takes three months to reach its extreme northerly path in late June. From its fall equinox path it drifts slowly southward for three months, toward its extreme southerly path in late December. In late June the sun will rise northeast and set northwest; in late December its arc extends from southeast to southwest.

At any time of the year, the sun is true south at its highest point (as is the moon). For someone at the center of a time zone (in an east–west sense), the sun is directly true south at noon standard time, and that person's shadow will point true north.

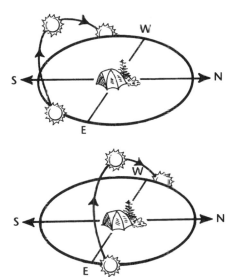

The sun's path:
top, *in mid-December;*
bottom, *in mid-June.*

This varies a little with your position in your time zone. If you're east of the center, sun events happen at an earlier clock time; west of the center they happen later. Time zones are spaced at longitudinal intervals of approximately fifteen degrees around the globe. The sun moves fifteen degrees an hour, crossing one whole time zone.

Here's how this works out. If you're hiking near the eastern edge of your time zone, say 7 degrees east of its center, the sun will be true south seven-fifteenths of an hour sooner, or twenty-eight minutes *before* noon standard time (it takes four minutes for the sun to move one degree).

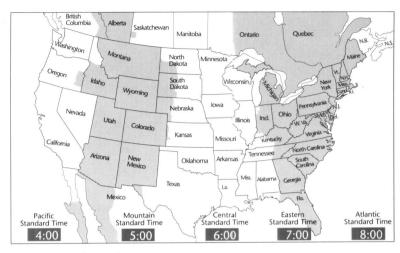

North American time zones

A rough notion of direction can be had by the old stick-shadow method, based on the westward motion of the sun. This is most accurate around midday. Stand a straight stick at least 2 feet long upright in the ground (the longer the stick, the faster this works). Mark the top of the shadow. In a few minutes, when the sun has moved west and the shadow has shifted noticeably eastward, mark the tip of the new one. Make one or two more markings as the shadow moves. A line connecting the marks will run east and west, with west being at your first marker. A line perpendicular to this one will run north and south. This method is rough; it produces a straight line only around mid-March and mid-September, and arcs the rest of the time.

If you have a nondigital watch, it can be used with the sun for a rough direction estimate. Set your watch on standard time (move it back an hour if you're on daylight saving time) and face the sun. Hold the watch horizontally and point the hour hand at the spot on the horizon directly below the sun. South will be halfway between the hour hand and twelve o'clock. This method is based on the fact that the hour hand moves 30 degrees an hour, twice as fast as the sun.

What matters to the outdoor traveler is not official sunset time, but **how much daylight is left** at a particular location.

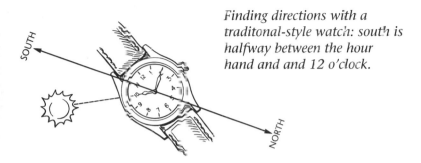

Finding directions with a traditonal-style watch: south is halfway between the hour hand and and 12 o'clock.

Use the following method in late afternoon to find out.

Fully extend your left arm in front of you with thumb pointed up, fingers extended together and palm angled toward you. Move your arm until the sun rests in the corner of the L formed by your palm and thumb. Now observe the vertical distance from there to the point on the horizon where the sun will disappear in terms of finger-widths (remember that the sun will continue to angle a bit to the right as it sets). Each finger-width represents about fifteen minutes of daylight, so if the distance is four fingers you have approximately one hour until the light dims and the air chills. If sunset is more than an hour away, you'll need to enlist the aid of your other hand.

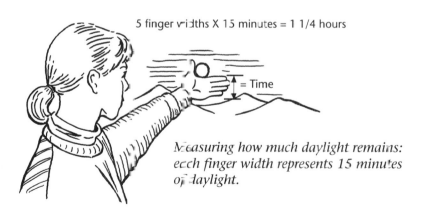

5 finger widths X 15 minutes = 1 1/4 hours

= Time

Measuring how much daylight remains: each finger width represents 15 minutes of daylight.

This same method can help you determine morning clock time if you know roughly when the sun rises where you are, didn't bring your watch, and happen to sleep later than you planned. Using your right arm, do the arm and sun trick toward the easterly sun to figure out how long it's been up and add that span of time to the time of sunrise to get the current hour. You may need to revise your hiking goal for the day!

Estimating Time by Sun Bearings

Based on the fact that the sun travels fifteen degrees an hour across the sky, a rough notion of clock time can be obtained by taking true bearings on the sun. This method is most accurate in the two-hour spans before and after noon, and even then may be off by up to thirty minutes. There are several complicating factors: often our horizon-to-horizon sky isn't an exact half-circle, and the sun doesn't make an arc directly overhead. In addition, bearings on the sun are much easier to measure when it rides low in the sky (as in winter) than when it is high overhead. But if you're hurrying to cross a glacier-fed stream before 11:00 A.M., as a trail log might suggest, this is better than no idea of time.

Even if there's no pressing reason, it's fun to estimate time this way, and if you choose not to wear a watch, you'll still have a good general idea what time it is.

Remember that the sun is true south, or 180 degrees, at noon standard time at the center of your time zone. To roughly estimate clock time between mid-morning and mid-afternoon, take a *true bearing* on the sun:

1. Point the direction-of-travel arrow at the spot on earth directly under the sun.
2. Turn the compass housing until your declination (or declination tape if you've added one; see page 49) lines up with the north-seeking end of the needle.
3. Read the true bearing at the index line.

What time is it? Figure out the difference between this bearing and 180 degrees. If the bearing is less than 180, subtract it from 180. If it's more, subtract 180 from it. In the illustration, the hiker with a declination of 10 degrees E gets a difference of 20 degrees (180 − 160). Divide the difference by 15. In that example, the sun is still 1⅓ hours away from its noon position (20 ÷ 15 = 1⅓), so clock time is roughly 10:40 A.M.

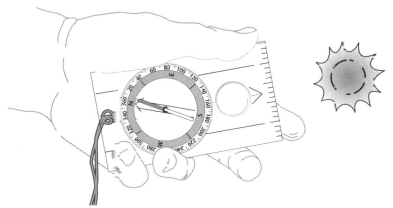

A hiker with a declination of 10 degrees east gets a true bearing of 160 degrees toward the sun.

In another place with a declination of 10 degrees w, a hiker finds the sun on a bearing of 210 degrees. The sun has traveled 30 degrees past its noon position (210 – 180 = 30) and the time is therefore approximately 2:00 P.M. (30 ÷ 15 = 2).

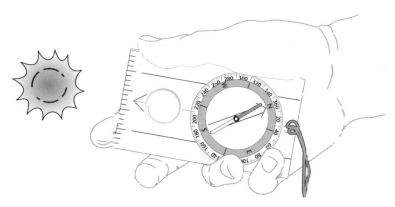

A hiker with a declination of 10 degrees west gets a true bearing of 210 degrees toward the sun.

These examples assume the hiker is at about the center of a time zone. That's close enough for this rough "clock." If you want more precision and enjoy fiddling, you can throw in a

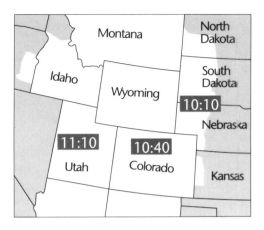

If a sun bearing yields the time estimate of 10:40, it would be adjusted to 10:10 at the eastern edge of the time zone, and to 11:00 at the western edge.

further adjustment. If you're hiking in an area *not* at the center, adjust the clock-time estimate accordingly (four minutes for each degree you are off the center of the zone). East of the center, where sun events happen earlier, *subtract* from the estimate; west of the center, *add* to it. (If you're not sure about your position in the time zone, look at a road map or the time zones map in a telephone directory.)

Where Will the Sun Rise?

Measuring true directions has a very practical application that can add a bit of luxury to your camping. Remember Carrie, who wanted to set up her tent so she'd wake with the rising sun shining in her door? Carrie knew from her understanding of the sun's seasonal path that it rarely rises and sets exactly east and west, that its arc usually varies either to the north or south of that line, depending on the time of year. At all but the east-to-west times, the sun doesn't set exactly opposite in the sky from its rising place. If it did, we could simply measure the true bearing to the point where the sun sets and subtract 180 degrees (a half-circle) to figure out where it will come up the next day.

Because the sun's path will usually be either "above" or "below" the east–west line, you can estimate its rising point by taking a true bearing on its setting point and subtracting that number from 360. The setting bearing measures the angle from the top of the earth. The rising bearing is the same-size angle; you simply flip the angle mathematically from left of the top to right of it.

Say it's late April when Carrie wants to figure out where the sun will rise. At that time the sun's path for the northern United States will be from northeast to northwest, and she's likely to get a setting bearing of 284 degrees or so. This is a bit north of west, and she can expect that the sun will rise a bit north of east. Subtracting 284 from 360, Carrie gets 76, the approximate *rising* bearing of the sun.

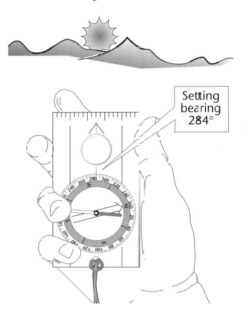

Setting bearing 284°

True bearing to the setting sun = 284 degrees

Remember, she's using *true* bearings because the sun moves in relation to true directions, not magnetic. Here's how she does it:

1. She points the direction-of-travel arrow at the place on the horizon where the sun will set.
2. She turns the compass housing until her declination (20 degrees E in this example) is at the north-seeking end of the needle.
3. At the index line she reads the true bearing, 284 degrees.
4. She subtracts 284 from 360, getting 76.
5. She now turns the compass housing until the rising bearing of 76 degrees is at the index line.
6. Holding the compass horizontally, she turns body and

compass until the declination is again marked off by the needle's north-seeking end.

7. She has pointed herself at the sun's rising bearing, and looks up to find that point on the distant horizon. Looking around the campsite, Carrie notes that a group of tall fir trees near the other tents will keep them in shade for an hour or more after sunrise, so she erects her shelter where there won't be any shadow makers between her and the sun.

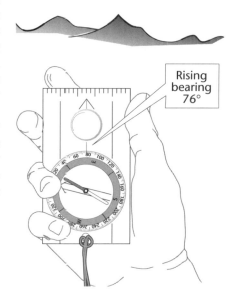

True bearing to where the sun will rise = 76 degrees

True direction to the rising and setting sun on the first day of each month for 40 degrees north latitude, an average for the United States. (The direction to the sun varies with your latitude.)

Month	Rising	Setting	Month	Rising	Setting
January	121°	239°	July	59°	301°
February	113°	247°	August	66°	294°
March	100°	260°	September	79°	281°
April	84°	276°	October	94°	266°
May	70°	290°	November	109°	251°
June	67°	293°	December	119°	241°

The Night Sky

Nighttime hiking is almost never wise, but if you've lost your compass you can use the stars to figure out directions, mark them, and make use of this information the next day.

Like the sun, stars rise in the east and set in the west, except for the stars that rotate around Polaris, the North Star, which never set.

Polaris, to the naked eye the only star that doesn't move, is never more than one or two degrees off true north. It's fairly bright, and most North Americans will find it about halfway between the northern horizon and the zenith (overhead).

You can locate Polaris in relation to either the Big Dipper (Ursa Major) or Cassiopeia. These constellations and the Little Dipper (Ursa Minor) all rotate counterclockwise around Polaris, which is the end star of the Little Dipper's handle. All three constellations can be seen year-round, so they're good direction finders. (Most constellations disappear beneath the horizon at various times of the year because of the tilt of the earth's axis.)

Polaris is about halfway between the Big Dipper and Cassiopeia. A line drawn through the two outer stars of the Big Dipper's bucket and extended about five times the distance between them will reach Polaris.

If the Big Dipper is hidden by clouds or a hill on your northern horizon, use Cassiopeia to locate Polaris. Roughly opposite the Big Dipper, its five brightest stars form a W, with the top always toward Polaris.

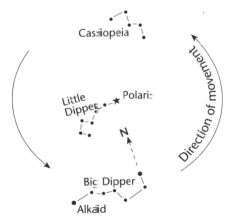

Find Polaris—nearly stationary and almost always true north—in relation to the Big Dipper or Cassiopeia, which rotate around it.

At least two other constellations can be used to find north. The top of Orion, a winter constellation in the northern hemisphere, is consistently toward the north, as is the back of Leo.

If clouds or the view from your campsite thwart efforts to locate Polaris, try to find east. Watch the horizon and see where the stars are rising. A few minutes of patient observation will give you the answer. Once you've determined which direction is east, north is to your left.

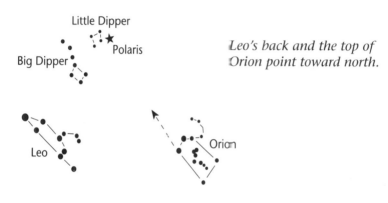

Leo's back and the top of Orion point toward north.

Vegetation

Vegetation growth follows some *general* directional rules, but conditions such as local weather and the shape of the land are always complicating factors. Take general clues from observing the green things, but don't rely on them except as a last resort.

In the northern hemisphere, north and northeast slopes get less direct sun in a day than south-facing ones, and hence are cooler and damper. In general the vegetation on north-facing slopes is greener and richer, and snow and ice will last longer.

Does moss *really* grow mainly on the north sides of trees? Generally it may be thicker there, but you can find moss growing on any and all sides of trees because of the climate in a particular spot.

Route Planning

Where to Go?

Your first itch to explore an area might come from friends, an enticing description in an outdoor magazine, a hint from the outdoor-store clerk, or from studying unknown territory on a map.

If there are regional offices for the Forest Service or Bureau of Land Management in your vicinity, pay them a visit. They can sell you maps and provide current information about the wild places they oversee. Because these agencies are trying to combat overuse of a few popular areas, they're glad to steer you toward fine spots that are less well known.

Wilderness areas, the most use-restricted of our backcountry, are designated by Congress and found within publicly owned lands. The managing agency will be able to tell you which parts of a wilderness area are likely to yield solitude.

Within each Forest Service region are anywhere from one to twenty national forests full of hikeable country. Each national forest has a supervisor's office (look in the telephone directory under United States Government, Department of Agriculture), and this is another source of ideas about where to go. In addition to maps, you can sometimes obtain detailed trail logs (mile-by-mile descriptions) to help plan your trip.

Your state, too, may have extensive forest lands under its supervision, with offices that can suggest places to wander.

Along with maps of your trip area, find out if there are any use restrictions and if a permit system is in force. You need to know if the number of campers is limited at a lake you want to visit. Sometimes whole areas are temporarily closed due to high fire-danger levels. A bridge on your route may have been washed out. Your favorite alpine camping area may be restricted, cordoned off, and replanted in an effort to restore trampled vegetation. The local ranger or his counterpart is usually the best source of current information about road and trail conditions and the like. Some outdoor stores post current National Forest Ranger District reports. Some along with libraries and regional Forest Service offices, have terminals for computerized trail information systems.

In settlements near your trailhead you can often ferret out verbal descriptions and suggestions from the townsfolk. Frequently this is sound and helpful, and leads you to some gem of a place you would otherwise have missed. But weigh this kind of advice carefully. All too often a description of the trail and country comes from the fond but distant memory of one who was last there twenty years ago.

Bookstores, travel stores, and outdoor stores carry a proliferation of hiking guidebooks that can supply enough trip ideas to fill every remaining weekend of a long and vigorous life. These books give abundant details about the hikes proposed, including which USGS maps cover the area, how to get to the trailhead, hiking times, available water, and, sometimes, interesting geological and historical background. Indeed, such descriptions are often so vivid that you can almost count on finding any publicized trails crowded with other folk who have succumbed to the printed lure.

Avoiding the Crowds

Plan your trips for times other than weekends, holidays, and the peak hiking season. Go to spots more than 5 miles from a busy trailhead, or enter a popular area from the least used side, away from major population centers. Choose areas away from tourist attractions, big campgrounds, and major highways—a few miles of unpaved road to a trailhead deter a lot of people. Avoid lakes easily reached by trails.

Stay off major, well-publicized trails such as the Pacific Crest Trail and the Appalachian Trail, at least at peak times. Explore lesser known secondary trails. Likewise, wait awhile to visit areas recently written about in newspapers and magazines.

Detailed Map Study

Take a close look at the topographic map *before* you pack up to hit the trail. It can give you all manner of information related to planning an itinerary. Even for a hike done entirely on trails, a map helps.

- The map will preview just where the trail goes and show some of the treasures and obstacles along the way—a great ridgetop view, a challenging water crossing.
- Elevations can tell you where you might encounter lingering snows in early summer, and where a late October walk could include dusting by early snowfall.
- The patterns of contour lines will tell how steep a stretch of trail will be, how hard the climb between two points, and will help estimate travel time and set realistic goals.
- You can figure out likely water sources from map symbols and the season of your hike, so you'll carry enough, but not too much, water—one quart weighs two pounds!
- A look at the topography may suggest special travel equipment you'll need: ropes to aid in difficult water crossings, ice axes for a high exposed pass on an early season trip, tennis shoes for fording streams.
- Knowing a buggy swamp lies on your route, you can plan to travel past in the cool morning hours.
- A map will alert you to glacier-fed streams that should be crossed early in the day before they swell.
- Map study provides a view that walking the trail can't: a look at the *whole* piece of land the trail is just one part of.

Other Planning Matters

What's the likely travel time for each leg of your proposed route? On moderate trails, carrying an average load, you may travel about 1.5 miles an hour, including rest stops. Steep climbing is much slower, of course; so is hiking in very hot weather. How far or fast you move is an individual matter best determined by your own experience. This has to do not just with the kind of country you're traveling over, but with such factors as weather, group pace, and the purpose of the trip. Don't be surprised if you discover that your actual hiking time differs substantially from the estimates given in guidebooks.

Remember that the first day's goal should be conservative. That's when loads are heaviest, people possibly out of shape and acclimatizing to higher elevations. Hikers may not be well rested, having been up late packing or too excited to get a restful night's sleep. Perhaps a long drive precedes the first day's hike. At any rate, always allow for a margin of time and energy reserve. If you are set on camping at a special spot and reach it two hours sooner than expected, you can always use the extra time exploring the neighborhood. But it's bad news to trudge on with fading light and energies toward a rigidly held goal.

When you're sizing up possible routes, consider what the terrain will be like at this particular time of year. For instance, a large stream-threaded meadow at 6,200 feet will be swampy and buggy for several weeks after the snows recede, but in late summer and early fall it might make an idyllic base camp.

A frequent seasonal problem is the availability of water. I learned one very long and thirsty late summer day how much care is called for in map scouting the water supply. Assuming there was water in the small ponds shown high on a long ridge, I carried almost none. To camp near water that night, I hiked several miles farther than originally planned.

Planning Off-Trail Travel

Map scouting is twice the fun when you're ready to forsake the well-trod paths. Test your map and compass skills and build confidence with easy hikes under favorable circumstances. Make your first off-trail (cross-country) trips during good weather, in varied terrain with distinctive landmarks that provide ready route-finding clues.

How about a weekend trip on a route that uses trails part of the time but also takes you into easy trackless terrain? Or a base camp near a trail, with off-trail daytime probes in different directions? You might try cross-countrying in an area enclosed by a loop of trails or a valley between two ridges. Maybe there's a lake whose outlet you could follow for a mile or two until it crosses a trail.

A sense of the big picture is always important to a wilderness traveler, but it is absolutely crucial to one who leaves the trails. Because the land itself is your guide, losing sight of landmarks in poor visibility has more impact than it does on the hiker who can still see his path and trail signs. It's essential that the cross-country walker be constantly aware of the *total* scene and his place in it. Then, if the larger picture shrinks in a fog or whiteout, he can alter course appropriately.

Prior map study should include looking for possible alternate routes and baseline features that could provide a way out if the need arose.

You'll need to estimate mileage yourself for the legs of a cross-country trip, since the map won't supply it in neat figures along a trail line. A map measurer rolled along your route will give a rough estimate. Another way to measure your route is to lay a piece of string along it, then stretch the string out along the map's bar scale. For steep country, increase your estimate by 15 to 30 percent to get a more realistic notion of how far you'll walk. The map's red public-land survey lines can give you a rough idea, too. Each time you cross one section, you've moved about 1 mile horizontally.

Off-trail hiking is usually slower than walking on trails, but it isn't necessarily always difficult going. You might travel through mature forests with little undergrowth, along a gentle ridge above timberline, across an open desert. If your route goes through woods with thick underbrush, on the other hand, count on taking up to three or four times longer to cover the distance than you'd need on a trail. In planning a trip, keep your goals conservative as to time and mileage; this will eliminate pressures that can nudge you into unwise choices as you travel. Cross-country can be great fun, but it may not go as expected—and the unpredictability is one of its appeals. You should have slack in both time and energy to allow for unexpectedly slow or difficult parts of your journey.

One factor that's crucial to an off-trail hiker is that the surface cover on white areas of the map is often a mystery until you actually see the land. And what covers the ground directly affects the person who traverses it without benefit of trails. Ground surface or cover, combined with the shape of the land, determines the ease or difficulty of travel through it.

A flat area might be dotted with scratchy sagebrush. A formidably steep slope could have a new trail that zigzags right to the top—good reason to gather all possible current information—or it could be clothed in scree (small, loose rock) that makes for a slow climb up but an easy, fast descent. Talus (larger rocks) might either slow you down considerably or be easily negotiated by boulder hopping.

You've picked the area and some particular spots you want to visit. How do you decide on a route? A basic rule is to pick an *energy-efficient, safe course.* First plot the straight course between points, then study what the map says about the terrain for the best way. Realize that the nearest, most direct route is often neither easiest nor best. Skirting a big brushy flat or going around the head of a tangled ravine may increase the distance but decrease the time. Avoid fighting your way along brushy streambanks, slogging through swamps, climbing and descending slopes unnecessarily. Go around obstacles such as vast areas of wind-downed timber or dense scrub.

Make use of the lay of the land rather than superimpose a rigid, straight course over it. If you decide to depart from the original bearing line, take advantage of natural routes such as draws, gentle slopes, and clearings shown on the map. Plot bearings for short legs of the hike if they are at all unclear. Move along at the same elevation, or "contour," around hills in your path instead of going up and down simply to maintain a bearing.

Consider whether slopes face north or south. Depending on the season, you might want to avoid much travel on north-facing slopes where lingering snows or thicker undergrowth would make the going more difficult.

When picking your course, take both a short- and long-range view of the options. The way that looks easiest in its early stretches may get you into problems later on. When possible, aim for a large or long destination such as a ridge, stream, or long lake instead of a point. And use intermediate goals as checkpoints along the way; the risk of missing your destination increases with the distance traveled.

When It's Over

You can learn a great deal about route finding with each cross-country trip. After it's over, retrace on the map your actual route, evaluating how the trip went and learning from both your successful choices and mistakes. Challenge and skill sharpening are among the delights of off-trail travel.

Staying Found

With 4 miles and an elevation loss of 1,600 feet to go, a friend and I savored a coming-off-the-ridge view of several lakes that lay at the base of the mountain. This was our fourth and last day of sampling part of the Pacific Crest Trail that traverses Mount Jefferson and Three Fingered Jack in the Oregon Cascades. This year a major rerouting of a section had been completed, taking travelers high across the side of Jack rather than through lower lake basins suffering from years of heavy use.

Rounding a turn at an easy clip, we stopped abruptly and blinked. A group of college-age kids huffed and puffed

up the ridge, toting a rubber raft, a six-pack of beer, and little else. Without a map, they had started up this sparsely signed new PCT thinking they were headed for the lakes; in reality the closest water was 10 tough miles from the trailhead.

Bartering a map for a couple of beers, we helped them sort out their choices: a long backtrack or a shorter but tougher cross-country stint. In either case, a day of gentle lazing in the boat was not to be.

Why Do People Get Lost?

First, let's define *lost*. You are lost when you don't know where you are *and* you don't know how to get where you want to go. Not knowing exactly where you are is not the same as being lost.

Rare is the hiker who has never been at least temporarily confused, unsure of his location if not actually lost. When people get lost, usually one or more of these reasons is involved:

- They don't know the territory, and don't do the map homework needed to start with a mental picture of the area.
- Their knowledge of the route isn't current enough; trailheads and access roads change, trails are rerouted or cease to be maintained.
- They rely on the navigational know-how of a companion who is in the process of getting lost himself.
- They travel without a map because the route seems obvious, a sin that casual day strollers are guilty of more often than overnight walkers.
- They daydream and miss junctions or wander off on animal trails.
- They rely on their nonexistent "sense of direction," even trust instincts over compass.
- When adverse circumstances start to enter the picture—deteriorating weather and visibility, fatigue, flagging spirits, and dulled awareness—they charge ahead anyway.

The many specific things you can do to increase your chances of staying found can be grouped according to the places you consider them:

- before you leave home
- at the trailhead
- on the move
- around camp

Staying Found Starts at Home

Head for your trip with a happy body and a brain ready to function efficiently. If you are taxed by lack of sleep, a bad cold, a hangover or a recent bout with flu, or preoccupied with stressful problems at home or work, then your best route-finding equipment (*you*) is weakened before you're out the door.

Be sure you understand the rudiments of map and compass use *before* your trip. Applying and firming up these skills in the field will be much easier if you don't have to start from scratch. Be sure to *pack* map and compass, along with a pencil and paper for making notes on your route, plotting bearings, and leaving emergency messages.

Once you've decided on a route, highlight it on your map with yellow felt-tip pen (you can still see the details). This will save time and possible errors in reading, especially when you're tired or making a quick map check in rain.

Study recent maps of the area to get as complete a mental picture as possible. Look at topographic maps for information about the planned route: its directions, elevation changes, landmarks you should see as the hike progresses. But go beyond the narrow aisle your trail occupies to get a feel for the big picture, the general lay of the land. This increases your range of alternatives once you're out there and could be helpful if you need to depart from your original plan. Are there any big baseline features such as a river, a ridge, a road? What directions do they run? Where are they in relation to your route? Consult a road map for clues about the surrounding country that could be useful in an emergency. Where are nearby towns and roads? How far away? In which direction?

Augment map study with information about current trail

conditions and routes from others who have been there recently, up-to-date guidebooks, and a call or letter to the local ranger or equivalent. Lingering snow may still cover the trail on the highest section of your planned hike; the first mile may have been rerouted because of overuse. It's better to know about changes such as these *before* you're wandering around trying to figure out what happened and where you are.

Without fail, even for a day hike, **leave a written itinerary** with some responsible person (who likes you). Should you run into trouble, this one act could save crucial hours or days. If you are lost, feeling assured that someone knows where to look and will soon be searching for you can keep panic in check. Leaving an itinerary is doubly important if you will be hiking cross-country.

In addition to *telling* your friend where you plan to hike and pointing it out on a map, *highlight* your route on a copy of the map or *write it out*. In an emergency the brain often fails us—"Was it Devil's Peak or Angel's Peak they were going to climb?" Your note should include the following:

- names and emergency telephone numbers for group members (relatives or neighbors, for example)
- description and location of vehicle(s)
- departure and expected return times
- route, with likely campsites
- alternate route and the circumstances under which you'd use it
- list of visually distinctive equipment
- whom to contact (county sheriff, district ranger, or other rescue personnel) if you're overdue, and how long to wait before calling for rescue (when you return, be sure to check in so your friend knows you're back!)

Group size has a bearing on staying found. Do you plan to hike alone or with companions? Although solo hiking may sometimes be your choice, recognize that your chances of getting lost are usually much greater alone, and act accordingly. Since there is no one else to correct route-finding mistakes when you travel alone, use extreme care in planning and following your route.

On the other hand, an unmanageably large group can get

strung out and lose someone who lags behind, goes off the trail for a bit, or stops to smell the flowers. The family-sized group that the Forest Service now recommends for low ecological impact also makes sense for staying found.

At the Trailhead

Review road and topographic maps to fix in your mind a picture of the area. Orient the map, identify prominent landmarks and their directions from the trailhead. Note the compass bearing for the first stretch of trail. These bits of information could help you get back to your starting point.

If for some reason you decide at this point on a route change (perhaps car trouble on the way has trimmed available walking time), try to call home. If that's not feasible, at least leave a note on the dashboard indicating the change.

Some people advocate always leaving an itinerary note with the car telling where you'll be and your departure and return times. Unfortunately, trailhead vandalism is not unheard of, especially at very popular takeoff points. To announce your length of absence could sometimes invite trouble, so weigh that possibility.

On the Move

Keep map and compass handy so you can get at them without removing your pack—you'll use them more often. Your shirt or parka pocket might be the place, or an outside pack pocket within reach. If your pack doesn't have this feature, you can easily sew on a simple map pocket.

Some folks like to wear a small beltpack that houses items for use while traveling, includ-

A map pocket you can reach while wearing your pack will encourage you to use the map.

ing map and compass. It's a good safety measure to attach a cord to your compass and maybe run it through a buttonhole or around your belt. If skies are damp, be sure your map is protected from moisture in some way or your route could disappear in a soggy fold. Pencil and paper should also be close at hand.

If group members have varying levels of route-finding skills, the more experienced navigators should use the opportunity to train others. *Everyone* needs to be an active route finder, not just the first person in line or the one who has logged the most miles. Even a conscientious leader can miss a turn.

Whenever you consult your map, hold it so that it matches the landscape at least approximately, with the top toward north. It is easier to visualize where you are and what you're doing if your brain doesn't have to go through "turning things around." This simple precaution might also sometime keep you from making a left turn at a trail junction where you should turn right.

Is This the Trail?

Trails are marked in various ways. **Blazes** are carved from tree bark about 4 to 8 feet off the ground in the shape of a diamond, a T, a dotted I, or something similar. You'll usually find a blaze on both the coming and going sides of trees, which are blazed at close enough intervals so you can spot the next one without moving far. The following are a few cautions about blazes:

- Old blazed trees fall.
- Trees sometimes blaze themselves, when one falls against another.
- Occasionally lost hikers carve blazes that might later confuse your situation.

On some trails you may find small **metal plates** with a trail symbol, instead of or in addition to blazes.

Cairns, or "ducks," are manmade piles of rock that mark routes above timberline, through meadows, and in other unclear or treeless spots. Sometimes those at high elevations are swept away by avalanches; if you find a damaged cairn, try to rebuild it.

Blazes carved at eye level are the most frequently used trail markers.

Trails are usually "brushed out" to a height of about 8 feet. If you examine the trees on both sides of a trail you'll frequently find neat manmade **prunings** where limbs that would have stuck out into the path were trimmed. A saw or an axe leaves a smooth, even cut; when an animal chews or pulls a branch off, the scar is jagged or uneven.

A **worn tread** itself is the trail evidence most often relied on, but the day is bound to come when you wonder if you've strayed onto an animal trail. The worn track is still there, but things don't feel quite the same as on a people trail. Deer trails are much narrower—about the width of your spread hand. Where logs lie across human paths, people usually cut through or move them aside. Deer easily move over such obstacles. You'll probably need to duck to avoid brush and limbs that clear a deer's back easily.

An elusive trail on a slope will sometimes become clear if

you look for the **terracing effect** where the path was cut into the hillside. If your travels take you on trails overgrown by brush, a bit of ground-level searching may disclose the path itself, free of greenery. Compacted earth takes a while to bounce back to a natural vegetation pattern.

Trail signs made of wood can be reduced to an unreadable state by vandals or gnawing critters, flattened by snow, or carried off. I've seen junction signs turned the wrong way, like street signs after Halloween. Mileages on signs should be accepted as rough estimates; trust your map more for this information. There are plenty of reasons to have more than trail signs in your repertoire of route-finding aids.

Be particularly alert in circumstances where it's easy to lose the trail—reentering the trees after crossing a clearing; going back and forth over streams in a lush draw or canyon bottom; early-season hikes before the trail-clearing crew has been through and while snow patches may still cover an occasional stretch (sometimes masking a turn). When the trail eludes you for the few yards immediately in front of your boots, look farther ahead; it may be clearly recognizable.

The Key to Knowing Where You Are is Constant Awareness

What kind of terrain are you passing through? How is the landscape changing as you travel? Are you moving up a valley, traversing a ridgeline between two watersheds, skirting the base of a massive butte, paralleling a tributary to its junction with another stream?

Think of the landscape as a whole, fitting in new features as they come into view and as you anticipate them from frequent map checks. Break out of the tunnel vision that a trail and rhythmic footfall ahead can induce. **Look everywhere!** Notice close and distant landmarks, thinking about how they would look from other directions. Frequently **look back** where you came from, since that view is different and you may need to retrace your steps. Pay special attention to crucial junctions and turns.

Maintain constant orientation so that you are never unsure of where you are. Every fifteen minutes or so (more frequently in cross-country travel) match map and landscape, taking compass bearings if visual inspection alone doesn't yield a solid comparison. Pull out the map every time you reach a pass, junction, or new view, and whenever you have the slightest uneasiness about your location.

Keep track of what direction you're moving in, how far you've come, and approximate travel times. Be alert to **catching features** that tell you when to change course or leave a line. Note the distance between points so you'll have a general notion about how long you should expect to travel on given sections of your route. Be aware of changes in direction, always thinking of your progress through the landscape: "After a quarter mile of going west toward Shelf Rock, we turned north and are now paralleling the valley floor about a third of the way up its east wall, heading for Goat Pass."

A landmark isn't just an impressive peak; it is anything you can note and recognize later: a meadow, trail, cairn, remains of a shelter, gully, distinctively shaped butte, saddle between two peaks. Even a bearing to the sun at a certain time can be considered a landmark, since you could use that information along with other clues to establish your location later. In thick woods, don't count on trees as landmarks, even oddly shaped or large ones. Instead, use the shape and slope of the land, or things external to the woods: a river, distant peak, ridge.

If landmarks aren't visible because of bad weather or darkness, then reliance on map and compass is especially crucial. Don't stay uneasy about where you are for more than a few minutes. If you're that unsure, better to sit tight until visibility improves than to compound your dilemma by uninformed travel.

Whom Can You Trust?

Sometimes your instincts about direction will conflict with what the compass says, even to the point of being totally opposite. **Believe your compass**—*after* ruling out attraction by nearby metal and checking with other compasses in the group. Unlike migrating birds, human wanderers have no internal compass. We can work at developing a sense of direction, but mainly it will come from the continued careful observation of natural phenomena—vegetation patterns, the sun's position, and so on. Hone your observations by guessing which way is true north when your crew stops to rest.

The very types of terrain that are easy to get lost in can also lull a hiker into daydreams. When flat, featureless country, a fogged-in tunnel of a path, or dense woods are your trail lot for very long, your awareness can quietly click off without your noticing. Suddenly—as when driving across a desert on a hot day—you wake up and wonder how long you've been on automatic pilot and whether you passed that turnoff. The country you've come through during the lapse has left you with no route-finding clues; part of your equipment was shut down.

When traveling off trail, and if your route is unclear or complex for any reason, *always* whip out that pad and pencil and make notes, or even draw a map of your progress. Include landmark bearings, both ahead and behind, and travel times between points. Check off points on the map as you pass them, noting the time.

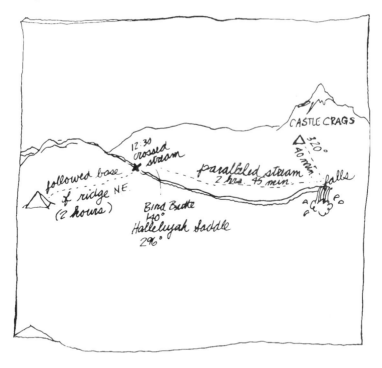

A route sketch is an invaluable aid to the off-trail traveler. Note route, travel times, and key bearings.

It is very easy to become disoriented when hiking in fog, overcast, or stormy weather. Check your compass frequently to make sure you are traveling in the desired direction.

If you ever feel you must mark your trail in order to find the way back—as on an overgrown trail in a fog or in some cross-country rambling—*don't* wound the trees with blazes. Instead, tie on strips of colored crepe or toilet paper, which will last long enough to guide you out but not much longer. On the way out, *remove your markers.*

Keep all members of your group within earshot of one another, and within sight if you're traveling off trail. Regroup at junctions, stream crossings, and at any confusing or crucial points. Anyone who needs to stop or leave the trail should tell someone else. It's easy to go ten yards into woods and lose your bearings, then head away rather than toward the trail.

Stay in good shape to ensure that your powers of observation and judgment will operate well. When fatigue sets in, it's time for a renewing halt. Dehydration can dull the mind long before you realize what has happened. Other physical problems can crowd your head. A hiker preoccupied with an untended blister or ill-fitting pack won't pay much attention to staying found.

There's no substitute for **active judgment** about a hike and all the factors affecting it—weather, how the group is doing, whether your pace matches what you anticipated, unexpected problems with gear, injuries, and so on. Be flexible enough to make changes if circumstances so dictate, rather than rigidly pushing on toward the original goal along the path you planned. That may have been great on paper, but it isn't worth the price you could pay in safety and comfort. Sometimes, turning back in the face of deteriorating weather or serious illness is the best choice. The country will be there for your next try.

If you make changes in your itinerary it's wise and sometimes possible to leave a note in a prominent spot, especially if you're alone.

A friend and I found such a message on a late fall hike. All day we had seen one set of large bootprints ahead, with dog tracks trotting faithfully alongside. Tucked in among the rocks of a junction cairn near camp that night we found this note in a plastic bag: "October 23, 1977. If you find this—I'm hiking alone from Frog Camp to Willamette Pass and am making a route change here. Instead of staying on the PCT to Island Meadow, I'm taking the trail from here to Horse Lake and Sunset Lake, to rejoin the PCT just north of Island Meadow. I expect to reach Willamette Pass October 28. Please notify the proper authorities. Thanks. (Name and address)." When we got home the next day we relayed the message to the district ranger and wrote the mystery traveler to say we'd found the note. Had this hiker's friends reported him overdue, his foresight would have given searchers a tremendous edge.

A plastic bag containing a note can be tucked into the rocks of a cairn.

Around Camp

As you approach your home-for-a-night and soon after you drop packs, cast a careful roving eye on the surroundings. Map and compass in hand, compare what you see with its topographic picture.

What is the shape of the land? Where is camp in relation to the largest peaks around? Are there any distinctive features you could spot if you wandered out of sight of camp? A rock outcropping? Cliffs? A group of unusual snags? A break in the ridgeline just west? If you are near a stream, note something distinctive a short distance away both upstream and downstream. Anything visible from a short distance will help. A friend once found his way back to camp in a huge canyon by heading for a big white blotch he had noticed on the wall above camp— a woodrat urinating station. By making a mental inventory of guides toward home (sometimes you might also want to jot a few notes in your pad), you are free to go exploring with an easy mind.

What to Do If You're Lost

Lost is too strong a label for those inevitable moments of disorientation or confusion, or for the many times when you don't know your exact location but don't feel lost at all.

Really lost is the predicament you can't work your way through in a few minutes, the situation that calls for resourcefulness and positive thinking. Few backpackers get really lost, unless they are extremely careless. And even being really lost rarely ends in tragedy. It may mean a day or two of discomfort while you await rescue—*unless* you lose your head and make things worse.

The greatest danger in being lost lies not in the weather or the country but in giving way to fear and panic. Keep cool, calm, and confident that you'll soon get found either by yourself or by others. A relaxed mind is better than a pack full of emergency gear; remind yourself that most lost travelers either find their way or are found within two or three days. Remember that itinerary you left?

If you think you are lost, *stop!* Sit down, calm down. Control fear so you can think clearly. Keep the group together. Look around. Yell, or better yet, blow a whistle. You can blow a whistle a lot longer than you can yell, with less energy, and the sound carries better. Listen for an answer: three is a distress signal, two a response. Should you hear those comforting two-toot responses, *stay put* as you continue to signal, so rescuers can home in on your location. Depending on the terrain, sounds can bounce around and be difficult to pinpoint. Competing wind or rain can also mask shouts and whistles, so keep signaling.

With oriented map at hand, pool all the information you have. Where were you last sure of your location? How long ago? If you've kept track of your progress you have at least a vague idea of your general location. After all, the top speed of a foot traveler can't take you very far off base very fast. Look at the country around you and examine the map for likenesses to the shapes and features you see.

Think back over the country you covered since your last confirmed location. You may decide you can retrace your steps in a relatively short time. If this is the action you take, mark the "lost" spot and take your pack with you. *Never* abandon your survival gear.

Look for prominent peaks, drainages, ridges, open areas. Use care and caution; wishful thinking can lead to a hasty misidentification of what you see. Even if you can take only one bearing to a known feature, remember that puts you *somewhere* on a line. Thinking of your rate of travel and last known location, you can probably estimate your position on the line by comparing the landscape around you with the map. If you sight *two* known landmarks, you're not lost at all.

If the spot where you stopped doesn't offer a view of the surrounding area, mark it with a cairn or with toilet paper, and seek a nearby high place, taking your pack with you. But don't risk injury by climbing a cliff or tree; being lost is enough to deal with. You may be lucky enough to top a rise and find a benchmark with a printed elevation. That rise will most likely be marked on your map. This higher view will usually tell you where you are.

If it doesn't, return to the marked spot and make short straight-line probes in different directions (gear with you), always coming back to the center. In all your searching, eyeball every tree and rock for evidence. You may stumble onto a section corner marker, if not a blaze or trail sign.

Is there a baseline you could head for? Consider the kind of terrain and probable distance to be negotiated before you would reach it. Remember that cross-country travel is almost always slower than trail walking. If the baseline isn't a quick or easy way out, at least it is a possible way. There may not be enough light left today, but perhaps tomorrow you could make it.

Sift all the evidence and don't travel unless you're sure of where you're going and there's plenty of daylight left. Don't follow a stream; many lead *away* from civilization rather than toward it. Resist the temptation to keep moving in the dark or in poor visibility. Getting hurt—cliffs, holes, creeks to fall in, windfalls to trip over—could make getting out even harder. If you do decide to move, leave a note giving your departure time, bearing, and destination.

Whatever actions you take while lost, conserve your energy for the cold and dark hours and the indeterminate interval until you are found. If you wear yourself out trying to get found, the possibility of trouble increases markedly: you won't be able to function in a strong and wise way, and will be much more vulnerable to hypothermia if things turn cold, wet, and windy.

Imagine two hours of daylight left and no good clues: time to settle in for the night. Make shelter in a protected spot, get water and lots of firewood. Don't fret if your food supply is skimpy; most of us could survive on our fat reserve for a long time. Water, however, is *vital*. A day without it will strongly affect most body systems; much longer guarantees serious trouble.

If settling in means you move away from a cold but exposed place, first put a visible marker there. A bright piece of clothing or an X of stones could attract attention.

Your shelter may be just a windbreak rigged from a poncho if you are on a day jaunt without full gear. If you have *nothing* to work with, look for natural materials such as logs, large boulders, slabs of bark, boughs (an emergency is the only justifiable reason for cutting them). A tree well can be the start of a serviceable shelter. Unless the country is tinder dry, build a fire. Huddle for warmth. Keep thinking about where you might be; you may get ideas to act on in the morning. Continue signaling at intervals.

In the morning, assess the situation again and decide whether to move—only on a *known* line toward a *known* destination—or stay put and await rescue. If you elect to stay, you can help searchers by getting out in the open, building a smoky fire, and blowing your whistle periodically. The hard-to-find person is the one who crashes blindly on in a panic, depleting energy with random movement.

After You're Found Again

Learn from your mistakes. Analyze what happened and why. Think what you could have done differently to avoid getting into trouble. Careful retrospection will fix in your mind how crucial small errors can be. You may even discover some persistent patterns in your way-finding habits that keep getting you into jams.

In the following examples of painful bits of learning from my more careless days, hindsight was a good teacher:

> The last day of a ski outing was marked by lousy visibility, so we were traveling entirely by close attention to the map and following short compass bearings. We turned south too soon and realized our error after about ten minutes of unplanned downhill travel into a creek drainage. We elected to continue in this direction, a choice that booked us for several exhausting and sometimes risky hours traversing a steep wooded hillside above the creek, frequently carrying our skis. It would have been much safer and easier in the long run to correct our mistake, climbing back to the original elevation as soon as we discovered our error.

> On our first venture into the high-desert Steens Mountain country of southeast Oregon, a friend and I learned why responsible, successful foot travelers use topographic maps. Relying on a planimetric map and verbal descriptions from the locals ("It will all unfold like a map as you climb!"), we couldn't find a crucial pass. Altering plans, we worked our way out of one canyon and found a narrow rim separating it from its neighbor. We had scrambled partway down the next canyon wall, much steeper, when darkness forced us to bivouac. Sleeping fitfully, we didn't know if or how we could get off the wall next morning. (We did.)

The lessons to be learned through post-adventure analysis add to your stock of way-finding skills.

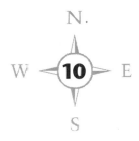

Teaching Kids to Stay Found

In hiking with your offspring, a major concern is to nourish in them the same staying-found skills you use yourself. Of necessity, young kids start out as passive travelers relying on the knowledge and authority of adults. If they receive just one small staying-found skill on each outing, kids will eventually become active route finders, staying found because of things they know and do of their own volition.

First, concentrate on teaching kids **what to do if they suddenly fee lost**: stop!

If they can't figure out where they are in a few minutes, they should make lots of noise and wait to be found. A whistle around a youngster's neck is a great comfort to whistler and whistlee. Be firm in insisting it is not a toy, but for emergency use *only*.

Toddlers are adept at slipping out of sight in a blink of the most vigilant adult's eye. As you hike, a youngster may be riding in a child carrier much of the time, but when a child is on foot around camp you can easily be distracted for a second, and that's all a disappearing act takes. A clanky bell pinned to the back of a little one's jacket could help you find him before he gets far.

At the start of each hiking season, review with kids the

basic staying-found techniques you've already imparted. Don't assume they'll remember from year to year. This review won't hurt you either.

Make sure kids follow this safety rule: let someone know if you need to sit and rest or if you want to go off the trail for any reason. Encourage them to call you on it if *you* abuse this rule.

Set and enforce camp activity boundaries. Don't, however, assume they'll always be heeded. A young child usually gets lost in the process of satisfying curiosity about things— chasing after a butterfly or squirrel, following a tiny stream, climbing over a rockpile to see what's in the cracks or on the other side. Children haven't yet developed an "adult" sense of insecurity about where they are or where they're going, so they don't naturally note landmarks or their place among them. Even with fairly old children, insist they do their exploring in sight of an adult or at least tell one exactly where they'll be.

Kids' early trips afoot are best taken in territory you're familiar with—and not in a jumbled confusion of forested low hills or a featureless, flat place. The latter are both easy to get lost in.

The small and close things of the world impress and intrigue a child, not the large-scale grandeurs we adults are awed by. A tiny waterfall you can crawl behind will win out over one 400 feet high across the valley. You can build on this fact of life when nurturing the incipient route finder in your child. Take advantage of this unquenchable thirst for small details—a person can't notice too many—and at the same time help children progress to noticing ever larger features of the land you're passing through. "This river is big because of all these little streams that feed it." (Point out the blue lines on the map.) "This little snowbank hasn't melted yet because the sun never shines right on it. It's the same with that big hill. On the south side the snow has melted; on the north side it's still there."

Frequently, and in as many clever ways as you can dream up, **be a model of constant awareness:**

- At rest stops and again at camp, play this game. "Look all around you, see as much as you can, big and little things. Is there water anywhere? Trees? Meadows? Hills? Cliffs? Where is the sun? Now close your eyes and talk about this place?" Kids will soon try to outdo each other and you in the amount of detail their word pictures include.

- Show kids how to recognize signs of a trail: blazes on trees, rock cairns, pruned branches, the worn path. Make a game of being first to spot the next blaze.

- As your hike progresses, point out a few plant features peculiar to where you are. Like unusual landforms, they can help children figure out where they are. "The beargrass was all bloomed out down where we started our hike; we've been climbing higher and here it's just coming out." "This forest is so shady, all that seems to grow under the trees is ferns." "See how the branches on all these trees are skimpy on one side and full on the other? The wind causes that."

As kids get along in years they should be reminded to think of a wild place in terms of the overall shape and features of the land. **Every detail they are encouraged to notice is a potential clue for staying found.** Learn (perhaps along with them) something of the geology of the region. Did glaciers carve this valley? Why is this headwall so steep and not eroded to a smooth and gentle slope? Was that line of rock rubble pushed off the mountain by a glacier? How did this cone-snaped pile of rocks form? Why is this meadow treeless, when the one we just passed had little pines growing in the lower end? How many colors can you find in the cliff face near camp?

Continuously give kids a progress report on where your group is and where it's going: "At the trail fork just around the next bend, we'll be halfway to camp... the next mile is all downhill. Then we'll have lunch where the trail crosses Windigo Creek.... There's a fork where a side trail comes down from Aspen Butte. We stay left."

Give older kids a turn at leading the group, with careful instructions not to get way ahead of the pack and to regroup at every junction, stream crossing, and maybe at the beginnings of steep stretches. Gently tutor young scouts in observing landmarks as they come into view and in frequently looking over their shoulders for a backward perspective. Before a child takes the lead, trace your route on the map with the young leader, teaching the rudiments of map reading a tiny bit at a time as you do so.

When you get to camp, take the kids in hand for a visual inventory of their surroundings. Direct their attention in particular to landmarks that stand out and could be seen by one who wandered away and got confused about how to get back. "See that cliff with the scraggly trees on top? That's right behind camp.... The only waterfall the map shows on this stream is *up*stream from camp, not far.... If you drew a line between that big mountain with snow on top and the lower one that's all reddish and bare, it would go right through our camp."

In the middle elementary grades kids are old enough to start learning the language of topographic maps. If you begin to introduce the simplest elements of this skill when kids are quite young, they'll be masters before they reach their teens. As with any area of learning, be careful not to turn beginners off by smothering them in too much information at one time.

Explain contour lines, the basic feature of a topographic

map, with the aid of a pond and a lumpy rock. The pond is "sea level" and the rock "a hill." Dip part of the rock into the water, then mark the waterline with a pen or pencil. Make a parallel "higher elevation contour line" by dipping the rock deeper and marking the new waterline. With your child, trace these lines over the rock's surface, showing how each line marks a given elevation above "sea level" whether it goes across a smooth part of the rock, around a bulge or into a dent. Now graduate to a nearby hill and compare it with its map picture.

At rest stops and quiet times in camp, play guessing games with your map.

- Start with the simplest symbols. How many streams can you find? Where is a swampy place? Is there more forest or open land?
- Move on to more advanced concepts. Which mountain is tallest? Can you find a hill with an unwooded east side? Will we hike *up* or *down* this steep part of the trail tomorrow? Here's where we are now. What mountain is about 1 mile ahead in the same direction we've been hiking?
- As your kids' map-reading fluency progresses they'll be ready to tackle harder questions. Does this stream flow into or out of Frying Pan Lake? How much elevation will we gain between camp and the junction with Horseshoe Trail? Can you find a good campsite about a day's hike north? Where would you put it if you were going to make a trail between Sunrise Lake and Marmot Pass, and why did you pick that route? By this stage they'll be firing questions in your direction.

At about the same time as you introduce maps, begin teaching the most basic compass operations. Kids love gadgets. Magnetic declination won't make sense for quite a while, but there are many things a hiker can do with compass alone, without adjusting for declination.

The main idea in these early years is to get kids familiar with the compass, its parts, the notion that a circle is divided into 360 degrees, and how to take and follow simple bearings. Then, as youngsters learn to use topographic maps, they'll eventually be able to put the two together. Even if compass skills extend no farther than orienting the map (which can be learned by rote before one understands declination), that single ability could help a child stay found.

Kids thoroughly enjoy finding north by their noontime shadow, with the stick-shadow routine. At night, teach them to find it from the Big and Little Dippers.

As the trail years with your family go by, encourage any budding interest kids show in route finding by giving them compasses and maps of their own. Maps showing country they've hiked themselves will seem special to them.

Key Ways to Help Kids

Your top priority is to teach kids what to do if they feel lost. Adapt the other aids—listed below, in ascending order for age and ability level—to your child's readiness and needs.

1. *Insist on two rules: let others know where you are, and stay within camp activity boundaries.*
2. *Explain how to get back to camp when it's out of sight.*
3. *Help your child notice detail (constant awareness).*
4. *Teach how to recognize a trail.*
5. *Give a continuous progress report as your group hikes.*
6. *Teach how to lead on the trail.*
7. *Teach the basics of map reading.*
8. *Show how to use a compass.*

Route Finding on Snow

We'd been skiing for four days since our last food pickup and contact with civilization, three-fourths of the way into a snow journey through Oregon's Cascades. It was demanding country for finding one's way—a couple of big peaks, which we couldn't always see, jumbled lower hills, and dozens of little lakes set in thick fir and hemlock forests. The day before, we had strayed too far west into an area filled with springs that undercut the snow and called for tense corrective maneuvers. This day we had a good ongoing notion of where we were, having identified several larger lakes. Still, when we set up camp it was recorded with a tentative X? on the map Reconnaissance probes after dinner located us right at map's edge, since nothing to the west matched any patterns on our paper guide.

You *can* find solitude, adventure, and beauty in the white seasons without going far, by making use of unplowed roads that are easy to get to. But finding your way around the winter landscape is usually far from simple. The minute you ski away from the prepared track, you *must* be a skilled route finder. Mistakes can cost dearly, not only in terms of basic safety, but in wasted daylight and energy. Both need to be more carefully monitored and rationed in winter.

Picture a trail brushed out to a height of 8 feet. Now put a

4-foot snowpack on that trail. The cleared tunnel through the trees is now only chest high and not nearly so obvious. To confuse matters more, you can see several other open places that could be the trail.

With trails and signs covered and blazes often covered or unrecognizable, the land itself is more your guide. But a coating of snow can make the most familiar piece of country seem foreign. Snowpacks of differing depths change the look of a place, as can drifts built up by wind, so even having visited a place once or twice in winter doesn't guarantee you'll always recognize it thereafter. Visibility is predictably poorer in winter, so it's often difficult to see landmarks at much distance. Like the cross-country summer traveler, the snowgoer must be constantly aware of location in the wider landscape and conscious of the direction of travel. Snowgoers must be even more self-reliant, able to handle the greater logistical problems of getting from here to there on a tricky, changeable ground cover—and skis are a bit harder to maneuver than legs. The consequences of route-finding errors are potentially more serious.

If finding your way around on snow is so much more difficult, why do it? Well, that's partly why—the challenge and satisfaction. And remember wanting to avoid crowds in the wilderness" Going in winter is a sure way, once you're out of sight of the parking lot and well-marked trails.

What's Different About Winter Wandering?

It's a whole new world out there. Besides the usual lack of trail and sign guidelines and generally poorer visibility, many other factors affect the winter navigator:

- Route and campsite choices are virtually limitless. One can often move right over brushy tangles that thwart hikers, and camp in meadows and on lakeshores without damaging the land.
- Because days are shorter and camp routines more time-consuming, there's usually less travel time.
- Some kinds of terrain take less energy to negotiate. Unless prone to frequent falls, going downhill is a skier's free ride.
- Some things can be harder work. Going up a steep hillside takes more energy for both skier and snowshoer.
- The pace of snow travel is much more variable, and often unpredictable until you're underway. It depends on more than just how much elevation is gained or lost in a mile, or how well the trail is maintained. How fast you cover a given piece of territory can change even in the course of a few hours, as snow conditions change.
- Several terrain hazards are peculiar to winter: tree wells, cornices, avalanche slopes, icy or crusty snow, bad ice on lakes.
- Water crossings can be much trickier and take more time. Sometimes, what could be safely waded in summer is simply uncrossable.
- Deciphering the landscape is frequently difficult. A flat open area could be a lake, meadow, or swamp. Drifts can hide small streams and make them look like snow-filled gullies. Drifts can also mask what in summer is a clearly defined lake.
- Good depth perception and an accurate assessment of distance are hard to come by when snow covers everything, and even harder with overcast skies.

Planning a Snow Trip

Until you've been out several times and feel friendly with the logistics of winter travel, keep your trips easy, conservative, close to help. Aim for the *least* mileage you could make in a day with poor conditions and use the slack, if any, for play. Plan to reach the day's destination at least two hours before dark. In December that could mean stopping as early as three o'clock.

Until you're there, it's very difficult to judge how much time it will take to cover a given piece of terrain. A heavy dumping of new powder snow, a rutted crust, or a warming trend that turns the snow to heavy mashed potatoes can make even road skiing tediously slow. Some nippy mornings you may find the snow so icy that it's simply unskiable for a couple of hours, but walking on it doesn't work either—you break through every few steps. Since temperatures and snow conditions are so variable and unpredictable, your route plan should be both conservative and flexible. If it isn't, you may pressure yourself into some bad decisions just to stick with the plan.

Learn all you can from map study at home so you can choose a route that avoids foreseeable hazards such as avalanche slopes. Avalanches usually happen on slopes of 30 to 45 degrees, but may occur on both gentler and steeper slopes. Sometimes the map will alert you by strips of white in larger green areas, marking where avalanches have wiped out the tree cover.

As you study the map for what might provide visual guides during your trip, don't plan to rely exclusively on features such as small streams or distant ridges. Both can disappear.

Pick terrain that's basically hospitable—gentle slopes, some open areas, distinctive landforms, not too many problematic water crossings. One of my favorite snow-camping areas is a lovely mile-square rolling plain, tree dotted and bounded on all four sides by hills and lava flows. They form an effective "fence" it would be impossible to cross unknowingly, even in thick blowing snow.

Locate a baseline or two. They can provide both boundaries to keep you from straying out of your chosen area, and lines you could follow to a given destination. Note how far you'd have to go for help or to evacuate one of your number, and in what direction. Lay out some alternate routes that could be used if needed. Is there a powerline cut or logging road you could use to reduce travel distance should the weather deteriorate?

Often winter travelers deliberately avoid trying to follow trails originally laid out for hikers. These trails tend to make frequent ups and downs, detour to scenic waterfalls, and cross high, steep areas for their great views. Such scenery is lovely, but not hospitable to snow travelers. You might plan a route that is near a hiking trail but hangs farther back from streambanks, whose undercut cornices can break away, or that skirts the edge of a lake basin instead of threading through it.

Planning a snow trip, you need to pay closer heed to water crossings, since you can't simply wade across; you might *have* to sometime as a last resort, but this chilling experience is best avoided. If your route takes in both sides of a sizeable stream, it may be essential that you find the one hiker's bridge over it, even though you don't want to be on the trail except at that point. If a stream is too wide to step across and doesn't have a sturdy snow bridge, you may spend considerable time locating a workable log crossing and negotiating it when you do.

If your snow trip is in an area laced with logging roads, be sure you supplement your USGS topographic map with the most recent Forest Service or Bureau of Land Management map showing roads. The snowpack may cover signs and road numbers, but such a map will still do a lot to lessen your confusion.

Gather as much advance information as possible about the area from others who have been there, outdoor stores, nearby resorts, the agency in charge of the land. These sources can fill in the picture with things a map can't tell you, such as the direction of the prevailing winds (which determine where cornices build up on exposed ridges), the snow depth, and which lakes are frozen over.

You might want to preplot your route and bearings at home, where your warm fingers work better. And be sure to protect your maps from the debilitating damp before you head out.

On the Move

Keep map, compass, paper, and pencil handy so you can make constant notes on your progress. Some people check off landmarks as they are passed. In general, follow all the rules that apply to off-trail travel, but with even greater care. If you keep good track of where you are, then a sudden reduction of visibility or mismatch of map and landscape won't cause panic. You'll be able to think back just a few minutes to when things did make sense.

Skiers and snowshoers often intend to stay on trails, but unless these are clearly marked as winter travel routes (with metal symbols 10 to 14 feet above the ground), doing so can be difficult. A snowpack of just a few feet may leave some blazes uncovered, but wind-driven snow readily fills in these carved depressions. To further complicate matters, that same blowing snow fills in natural depressions in tree trunks, making them look like blazes. This situation can occur, of course, whether the snowpack is deep or skimpy. So you can't assume that finding your way will necessarily be easier early in the season.

Even if you don't intend to stay on trails, it's helpful to be able to recognize one. Knowing when you encounter a trail is valuable route-finding information; it can help you figure out where you are (or sometimes, at least where you aren't). Lacking blazes and obvious cleared pathways, **prunings** are often the only clues to a snow-hidden trail. You'll find them low, sometimes even a few feet *below* ski level, in deep tree wells.

Many snow travelers grow careless about route finding, taking comfort in the idea that they can always follow their own tracks back to where they came from. This might work, but don't count on it. Just a few minutes of blowing snow can obliterate those tracks. And it's possible to confuse your tracks with those of others in the area. Depending on the snow and weather conditions, it's also sometimes difficult to distinguish between today's tracks and yesterday's.

Habitually make use of all available route-finding clues. Keenly observe terrain features both large and small, close at hand and farther away. Pay constant attention to the weather so you won't miss any brief moments of clearing. Fast-moving clouds may bare a crucial landmark just long enough for you to take a compass bearing on it and plot your position. Refer continually to the map.

By noticing *many* distinguishing features about your route and goals, you can avoid a lot of energy-wasting stumbling around. Are you headed for a meadow at the foot of a large peak? Look around and on the map for other clues about the area: a notch in the north spur ridge is above the border of the meadow; there's a stream flowing toward you from the other edge; between you and the clearing, the land makes a gentle rise bordered by two east–west draws.

The winter traveler especially needs to gather many route-finding clues—from observation and from the map—to keep on course.

Now, once you start for the meadow, you have several clues to keep you on course. Even if the tall peak disappears as your perspective changes or clouds lower, you might see the spur ridge, whose notch will tell you if you've come too far north. So would the draw on that side. And if you hit the stream on the left, you'll know to follow it to the meadow's south border.

Since you aren't bound to or lulled by a trail in winter, a feeling for the total landscape is both essential and inescapable. On a summer trail hike you may round the shoulder of a hill and hardly be aware of what you're doing. In winter, you make a deliberate choice to cover the country along certain routes.

Some terrain features present special problems. Streams

may be hard to identify. You can ski right over a frozen creek without realizing it, or be convinced that an empty gully holds a frozen creek. A lovely "meadow" may be a lake in white disguise, or vice versa. Positive identification may depend on noting the overall *shape* of an open area and the *nature of what surrounds it*, then finding the map's counterpart. Areas of deciduous trees that were green in summer—and still are, on the map—are now just bare sticks against a white background. You may have laid out a route through a forested area, only to find the woods too dense to get through.

If the map indicates a swamp or marsh but it's covered with a thick snowpack, it could still be unsafe to travel across. Decaying vegetation creates heat that melts the supportive snow from underneath. Undercutting can also happen around springs, near beaver and muskrat houses, and where streams enter and leave lakes.

Streambanks and snow bridges should always be respected for the possibility of undercutting by the moving water beneath them, even if it's just a few inches deep. On a smaller scale (but still potentially hazardous), check the thickness of snow around exposed boulders and logs. They draw warmth from the sun; the snow that looks solid may be melted thin from underneath.

Terrain features can be troublesome in more than the obvious ways of causing injury or a soaking in icy water. It's easy to be so intent on negotiating an icy hillside or dodging snowbombs crashing out of trees that you pay little attention to where you are and are going. Other possible sources of diversion include ski tracks, a glimpse of wildlife or signs thereof (such as still-steaming coyote scat or an enticing line of fresh bobcat tracks). Before you know it, you're no longer sure of your location.

The combination of weather and terrain can affect route choice. Plan stream crossings on snow bridges for the cool morning hours, when they're still firmly frozen. Even then, move several yards both upstream and downstream to get a good sideways look at the snow bridge you consider using. What looks sturdy from up close may be only a few inches thick.

A sudden warming trend and rain can swell tiny step-across creeks to raging torrents in a matter of hours. Warming temperatures, rain, and wind can also trigger the release of heavy loads of snow from tree branches over your head. In this situation, skiing a more open route is definitely safer and more enjoyable.

Low ridges between streambeds can sometimes provide good passage. There's less tangled brush, usually no avalanche danger, and frequently a better view of landmarks. But if the ridge is exposed and the day stormy, that's not the place to be.

Steep open slopes that spell avalanche danger sometimes call for wide detours, as do ridges with built-up cornices ready to let go on travelers below. You may have planned to ski across a lake that has suddenly started to thaw. Or perhaps the snow is just too icy on open shoulders along your planned route.

Any of the above situations could call for a deviation from your plan. When that happens, choose the easiest, most efficient way around, which is often not the shortest. If you have to deviate from the planned route to get around obstacles, measure the deviation by time and your speed of travel, adjust for uphill and downhill, and compensate back as soon as possible. If you've detoured twenty minutes to the west to get around a brushy area, you'll need to reverse not only direction, but the same twenty minutes to find the draw you were following. Be sure to keep track of things *as they happen* rather than in retrospect.

Be extremely cautious about traveling in poor visibility. Not only is it easier to get lost or hurt, it isn't as much fun.

The reality of snow travel is that it's often much less precise than dirt travel. For one thing, it's harder to move in a straight line on skis. For another, the speed of skiing downhill is often much faster than that of walking. This has two consequences related to route finding: it affects your ability to judge how much distance you've covered, and it lets you make bigger route-finding errors, faster.

The ease and pleasure of skiing downhill can also lure you away from a wiser but more difficult route. In one of my best-loved winter spots, I have to resist an inviting string of sloping meadows that I know ends above a rugged canyon, far from the trailhead.

Full of stimulating challenges, winter route finding will convince you that there's always more to learn.

New Year's Day was clear and bright as I skied toward Sisters Mirror Lake, hoping to be the first person there this year. My route led through a 0.5-mile-wide strip of deep forest that obscured the mountains otherwise keeping me on course. Compass in hand, I skied through the woods and emerged in the open, still on my travel line, no energy or time wasted. The recent deep snowfall lay unmarked except for a thread of coyote tracks ahead. The privilege of sharing this creature's lovely backcountry world was the kind of reward that makes route finding on snow worth the effort it takes to learn.

Appendix A

Alternate Method

This method makes frequent reference to the map's north–south lines. To get accurate results, you need to draw parallel vertical lines across your map at intervals of 2 inches or so. Do this at home before your outing. Take care that you can distinguish *your* lines from the not-quite-parallel vertical kilometer grid lines and public land survey system lines.

When instructions refer to "compass meridian lines" (not used in this book's main method), they mean the parallel lines printed on the bottom of the compass housing, to the left and right of the orienting arrow.

The following are the two basic rules for this method:
1. When measuring or plotting **bearings on the map**, never use the magnetic needle or the declination arrow.
2. When measuring or plotting **bearings in the field**, always align the magnetic needle with the declination arrow.

Adjusting for Declination

Either buy a compass with an adjustable declination arrow and set it to your hiking area's declination, or add a taped declination arrow yourself (see page 49).

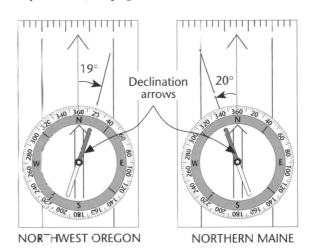

Compass declinations

19° → Declination arrows 20°

NORTHWEST OREGON   NORTHERN MAINE

The Basic Procedures

This method never requires orienting the map.

To Measure a Bearing on a Map

1. Place compass on map, with edge of base plate joining two points of interest, direction-of-travel arrow pointing toward goal.
2. Turn housing to align compass meridian lines with north–south map lines. (Be sure orienting arrow points to top of map.)
3. Read bearing at index line.

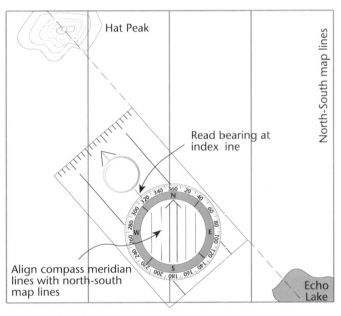

Measuring a bearing on a map

To Plot a Bearing on a Map

1. Set desired bearing at index line.
2. Place compass on map, with edge of base plate on feature from which you wish to plot bearing.
3. Turn entire compass to align meridian lines with map's

north–south lines. (Be sure orienting arrow points to top of map.) The edge of the base plate is the bearing line.

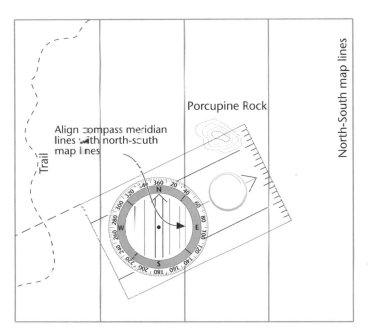

Plotting a bearing on a map

To Measure a Bearing in the Field

1. Set declination *first*.
2. Hold compass level in front of you and point direction-of-travel arrow at desired object.
3. Turn housing to align declination arrow with magnetic needle.
4. Read bearing at index line.

To Follow a Bearing in the Field

1. Set declination *first*.
2. Set desired bearing at index line.
3. Hold compass level in front of you and turn your whole body until magnetic needle is aligned with declination arrow.

4. Travel in direction shown by the direction-of-travel arrow.

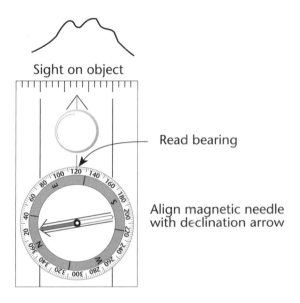

Measuring a bearing in the field

Applying These Procedures

Determining Your Position

If you know you are on one line (trail, ridge, stream, etc.):

1. Measure bearing to a known feature that is on your map.
2. Plot that bearing on your map. Where the bearing line intersects your known line is where you are.

If you know only the general area where you are:

1. Measure and plot the bearing to one known feature that is on your map.
2. Measure and plot the bearing to a *second* known feature that is on your map. Where the two bearing lines intersect is your position.

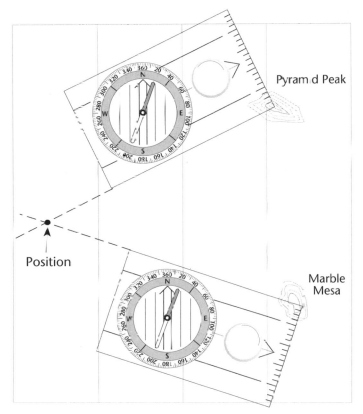

Pyramid Peak

Position

Marble Mesa

Plotting position by bearings to two known features

Identifying a mystery feature:

1. Measure the bearing to the feature.
2. Plot this bearing on the map *from* your known position. The bearing line will run through the mystery feature.

Finding a specific feature in the landscape:

1. Measure the bearing on the map from your position to the specific feature.
2. Hold the compass and turn until the magnetic needle is aligned with the declination arrow. The direction-of-travel arrow will point to the specific feature.

Appendix B

Whether in the sky, on the sea, or on land, GPS, the global positioning system, is changing how we navigate. GPS was developed by the U.S. Department of Defense for military uses. The system's twenty-four satellites circle the earth in high polar orbit. The satellites transmit radio signals that can be picked up by a special GPS receiver, which fits into the palm of your hand, weighs a pound, and runs for hours on a set of batteries.

A GPS receiver works by locking in on three or more satellites as they cross the skies overhead. The receiver computes its distance from each satellite by measuring the travel time of each signal. Through triangulation, the receiver determines its location. But a GPS receiver doesn't work alone, and it doesn't replace your map and compass and the skills needed to use them properly. Once you've determined the coordinates of your location, you need to consult a map with matching grids and units of measurement (USGS 7.5- and 15-minute topographic quads) and a compass to orient you. GPS works at night, in fog, in snowstorms, or in rain.

To work properly, however, GPS must be able to "see" the sky. Good triangulation depends on finding satellites spaced properly to zero in on your location. A cliff can cut off half the sky. A canyon can reduce the sky to a narrow sliver. It won't work if you are ringed by a high, heavy forest, or if you are in a cave.

In military form, GPS is accurate to about 30 meters. The Department of Defense, however, has degraded the civilian signal to where it is accurate to about 100 meters 95 percent of the time. Four percent of the time GPS is accurate to about 300 meters, and 1 percent of the time, the inaccuracy is greater than 300 meters. This intentional degrading is called Selective Availability.

GPS can also measure altitude, but Selective Availability has reduced the accuracy to about 147 meters. If we factor in poor triangulation caused by geography, the error could be greater.

These restrictions, though, are minor. As the receivers become smaller, less expensive (they're now $300–800), and more widespread, GPS use will be more commonplace.

Index

About the Author

June Fleming has taught and written about outdoor skills for twenty years. She leads backpacking and snow camping trips in the Pacific Northwest through the Portland, Oregon park bureau.

THE MOUNTAINEERS, founded in 1906, is a nonprofit outdoor activity and conservation club, whose mission is "to explore, study, preserve, and enjoy the natural beauty of the outdoors. . . ." Based in Seattle, Washington, the club is now the third-largest such organization in the United States, with 15,000 members and five branches throughout Washington State.

The Mountaineers sponsors both classes and year-round outdoor activities in the Pacific Northwest, which include hiking, mountain climbing, ski-touring, snowshoeing, bicycling, camping, kayaking and canoeing, nature study, sailing, and adventure travel. The club's conservation division supports environmental causes through educational activities, sponsoring legislation, and presenting informational programs. All club activities are led by skilled, experienced volunteers, who are dedicated to promoting safe and responsible enjoyment and preservation of the outdoors.

If you would like to participate in these organized outdoor activities or the club's programs, consider a membership in The Mountaineers. For information and an application, write or call The Mountaineers, Club Headquarters, 300 Third Avenue West, Seattle, Washington 98119; (206) 284-6310.

The Mountaineers Books, an active, nonprofit publishing program of the club, produces guidebooks, instructional texts, historical works, natural history guides, and works on environmental conservation. All books produced by The Mountaineers are aimed at fulfilling the club's mission.

Send or call for our catalog of more than 300 outdoor titles:

The Mountaineers Books
1001 SW Klickitat Way, Suite 201
Seattle, WA 98134
1-800-553-4453